KNITTING FROM THE TOP

BY BARBARA G. WALKER

A Treasury of Knitting Patterns
A Second Treasury of Knitting Patterns
Charted Knitting Designs
Knitting From the Top

KNITTING
FROM
THE TOP

By Barbara G. Walker

CHARLES SCRIBNER'S SONS / NEW YORK

3 5 7 9 11 13 15 17 19 Q/P 20 18 16 14 12 10 8 6 4 2

PRINTED IN THE UNITED STATES OF AMERICA
Library of Congress Catalog Card Number 72-504
ISBN 684-17669-6

ACKNOWLEDGMENTS

I am grateful for the warm encouragement of my editor, Elinor Parker, and for the help and support of my dear husband, Gordon N. Walker.

CONTENTS

Contents

KNITTING FROM THE TOP

Introduction

Most modern knitwear is designed to be made from the lower edge up to the neck or waist. There is a popular myth to the effect that working a garment in the other direction is much more difficult. This myth has been circulated not by knitters, but by instruction-writers—for the good reason that it *is* more difficult to write directions for such a garment, according to today's knit-by-numbers system.

Therefore the knit-by-numbers system is largely ignored by this book, which tells you in plain words, not in numbers, how to knit from the top down. Personally, I don't much care for numbers. They make me sleepy. I like to knit in my own way, thinking in terms of the happiest possible relationship between the garment and the body inside it. Despite the popular myth, I've found that knitting from the top down is an easy way to achieve this happy relationship.

Knitting from the top is easy because it insures a perfect fit with the barest minimum of calculating. Have you ever knitted a skirt from the bottom up, that came out too long, too short, too tight, or too wide? Have you ever knitted a sleeve from the bottom up, that stopped an inch short of the wristbone or else hung to the knuckles? Have you ever knitted pants from the bottom up, that either dragged on the ground or flopped above the anklebone? Length measurements are the trickiest part of knitwear design, because arms, legs, and torsos come in various assorted lengths, regardless of size. Designers may plan the upper portion of a garment to fit a body that is shaped differently from yours. No matter how carefully you have figured and measured the lower portions of your sleeve or skirt or coat, the upper portions—where you must follow the designer's directions—may be too long or too short for you, which throws off the entire finished length of the garment.

Knitting from the top takes the guesswork out of length measurements, and makes it possible for you to make all parts of your garment not just nearly right, but exactly right. You don't have to measure, and worry, and measure again, and worry some more. Having started at the top, you can simply try on the garment and look at it. It makes no difference whether you have worked just 3 inches of knitting, or 30 inches; you can try it on any time. The neck or waist portion, from which the whole garment hangs, and upon which all other measurements depend, is already there. Garments do not have to be taken off the needles to be tried on. An extra needle, or a length of string, can hold some of the stitches, so that the knitted fabric can be spread out for observation. When you are coming close to the length that you want, you can see—not just guess—how much more knitting should be done. You can bind off at the right moment, not a half-inch too soon or too late.

Another advantage of knitting from the top is that it leaves room for second-thoughts. If last year's skirt is too long or too short for this year's style, it is easily unraveled or knitted longer. Should you decide to shorten wrist-length sleeves to bracelet-length, it can be done in minutes. If your child is growing out of his or her sweater, you can add a few additional inches to body and sleeves. A garment knitted from the top down—especially a seamless one—can lead many different lives in many different lengths.

Some knitters believe that knitting from the top means just one thing: a seamless raglan sweater. But any style can be knitted from the top as easily as the classic raglan, with the same advantages of adaptable fit and neat construction. This book gives you a number of different basic styles, any of which can be used to make a garment for man, woman, or child, in fine yarn, medium-weight yarn, or heavy yarn, on any size needles. Once you understand the construction of any given style, you can make it to fit anybody, and use any material that pleases you.

This book doesn't tell you how to copy a knitted garment that someone else has designed. It tells you how to create your own. This is not so improbable as you may think. The subject of knitwear design has been made to seem much more mysterious than it really is, perhaps because many designers are unwilling to share their "secrets" with non-professional knitters. The truth is that to design your own knitwear you need only four basic tools: yarn, needles, a tape measure, and a brain fortified by a third-grade education; for it is usually in the third grade that we learn to add, subtract, multiply, and divide. There are no other arithmetical operations involved. So you can put away your slide rule, and forget all the algebra you ever knew.

Those who blindly follow commercial knitting directions may never have given themselves time to understand garment construction, so they remain always at the same level of untutored helplessness. Such are the people who have been knitting for years and years, but still say, "Oh, I have to have stitch-by-stitch instructions, or I don't know what to do." In fact the construction of a knitted garment is among the simpler things of life. Some of the world's most magnificent knitting has been done in past centuries by uneducated European peasants, who never went to school and could not read nor write, and whose acquaintance with arithmetic was rudimentary at best. They knitted to clothe the body, not to strain the brain. If they could learn to approach knitting from this angle, so can we.

The directions in this book are written from this angle. They are not at all like the directions you've been used to. They are neither abbreviated nor concise; they are long, rambling, wordy, and full of digressions, perhaps like the instructional style of a Lithuanian great-great-grandmother who knitted those incredible lace shawls that your family still treasures today. There is a purpose behind this windy manner of presentation. The purpose is to teach you not just *what* to do, but *why* you do it.

Each garment shape is achieved by direct, un-mysterious methods. When there are several possible methods for doing the same thing, alternatives are given, so you can choose the one you like best. Detailed instructions on various techniques are incorporated into the garment styles to which they are most relevant. Since this information may apply to other garment styles as well, you should read *all* of the basic designs no matter which one you want to start with. Here and there, just as when listening to that hypothetical great-great-grandmother, you may pick up bits of technique that are either new to your experience or superior, for some purposes, to your customary ones.

When you begin a knitted garment, your first creative act is to choose a pattern stitch or a combination of pattern stitches. The use of pattern stitches is the only really interesting thing about knitting; think what a bore it would be if someone passed a law stating that all knitters must use stockinette stitch only! The few diversions afforded by mere shaping would never be enough to retain the knitter's interest in her craft. But of course no one will pass any such law, and the variety of fabrics that knitting can make is literally endless. So, out of this immense variety, you choose; and having chosen,

MAKE A TEST SWATCH!

This is all-important; this is everything; you cannot design without it. In the first place, making the test swatch allows you to become accustomed to the pattern stitch, so you will know how it works, and consequently how to add stitches to it, or subtract stitches from it, when shaping. In the second place, the finished test swatch gives you the gauge (number of stitches and rows to the inch) that you will get with your yarn, your needle size, and your pattern. No one can discover this unique, individual gauge but you, and all of the measurements you make will have to refer to it. A test swatch should be at least 4″ square, or even larger. Making it is *not* a waste of time or a waste of yarn. It can save you many hours of backtracking and grief, and the swatch can be used as a patch pocket on the garment, or it can be unraveled to make use of the yarn, or it can be saved to serve as an afghan square one day. The test swatch is what tells you How To Calculate Shaping, which is all you really need to know in order to design your own original knitwear.

Shaping means to go from a larger width to a narrower width, or vice versa, by decreasing or increasing the number of stitches. It is usually desirable to have the decreases or increases (shaping units) evenly distributed between the two levels, as on the underarm seam of a sleeve, or in the taper of a skirt, or along the diagonal line of a V neck. There is only one question to be answered arithmetically: how many rows or rounds apart should the shaping units be placed? No matter whether you are knitting upward or downward, increasing or decreasing, the answer to this question is always discovered in the same way:

HOW TO CALCULATE SHAPING, IN FOUR SIMPLE STEPS

Step 1. Measure the width of the two levels, between which stitches are to be increased or decreased. For instance, on a sleeve, take the wrist measurement and the upper-arm measurement (allowing extra inches for ease, of course); on a skirt, take waist-and-hip, or hip-and-hem measurements; on a tapering sweater, take chest-and-hip measurements.

Step 2. Subtract the smaller of these two measurements from the larger, and multiply the result by your stitch gauge. This tells you how many stitches must be increased or decreased between the two levels. Then divide by the number of shaping units per shaping row or round. For instance, if you plan to increase or decrease 2 stitches at once, as is done on sleeves, divide by 2. If you plan to increase or decrease 6, 8, or 10 stitches at once, as is done on seamless skirts, divide by 6, 8, or 10. Write down the remainder if any.

Step 3. Measure the vertical distance between the two levels in question, and multiply by your row gauge. This tells you how many rows or rounds it will take to go from one level to the other.

Step 4. Divide Answer 2 into Answer 3. This tells you how many rows or rounds apart the shaping units must be placed. The remainder from Answer

·2, if any, can be worked as extra shaping units at the beginning, end, or anywhere along the way.

And that, ladies and gentlemen, is all there is to shaping. Did you think it was complicated? On the contrary, it's a sort of common-sensical problem-solving, on the order of "If Mary has ten apples . . .", etc. If numbers tend to make you sleepy, as they do me, you can always turn the shaping arithmetic over to the nearest third-grader—who, if he or she has been paying attention in school, can do it just as well as you or I can.

You have already perceived that shaping involves a certain amount of measuring. Throughout this book, the instructions tell you to measure "you", as if you were making every garment for yourself. But of course if you are making a garment for someone else, you take the measurements from that someone, and not from "you." If the wearer-to-be is not always handy, you can either measure a garment that fits him or her well, or take all the measurements from him or her at one time, when it's convenient.

When measuring from the body, remember always to allow for ease in the places where you want the garment to fit loosely. Never knit a sweater, for instance, to the exact width of the chest measurement. Such a sweater will be too tight. Allow from 2″ to 4″ extra here, depending on style and personal preferences. You must also allow for the movement of the body inside the garment. To demonstrate this to yourself, try this experiment:

Measure around your straight arm, exactly at the elbow. Pull the tape measure up firmly, but comfortably, and hold it there. Bend your elbow, keeping the tape measure right over the point of the bone. Ouch! It's like a tourniquet, isn't it? You wouldn't want your sweater sleeves to be like that. Loosen the tape measure to an easy fit over the bent elbow, then straighten your arm. You will see that at least 2″ or 3″ have been added to the original measurement. A sleeve has to have that width, or even more, at the elbow, so the arm inside can bend without seriously impairing circulation. When taking measurements from your own or someone else's body, remember that the idea is to knit a garment around the outside of that body, neither too close nor too far away. Hold the tape measure as loosely as necessary, and translate *that* number of inches into stitches according to your stitch gauge, because that's the number of inches you will get.

This measure-and-multiply method, combined with knitting from the top, is especially suitable for the hard-to-fit figure. The knitter does not have to depend on standard sizes. When you knit a garment from the top, there is none of that breathless waiting to get the last rows worked, the pieces blocked, and the seams sewn, before you can see whether the garment really fits. You know all along that it fits. And there are none of those nagging little disappointments in the final try-on, such as an unexpected tightness under the arms, or a depressing hint of sag in the front. It is entirely in your power to prevent disappointments like these. You, the knitter, are the master of a garment designed from the top down. It grows slowly, not as separate hunks of knitting, but as a garment—giving you plenty of time to criticize and correct. You don't have to sit there helpless while it becomes too wide, too narrow, too short, or too long. If it's too wide, decrease; if it's too narrow, increase; if it's too short, knit some more; if it's too long, unravel it to the right length. To make such adjustments, you don't have to go all the way back to the beginning and start over. You can take advantage of the wonderful adaptability of knitting, which shapes itself so obediently while it is being created.

Blocking and seam-sewing come under the general heading of Finishing, as do buttons, zippers, separate borders, facings, interfacings, reinforcements, linings, and other appurtenances aimed at pointing up and pulling together the final product. Many knitters are either too timid or too indolent to do their own finishing. Instead, they will pay someone at the yarn shop to do it for them. If you are one of those who dislike finishing, you will rejoice to learn that knitting from the top involves practically none of it. Each garment is an organic whole, almost from its birth. It puts itself together around the body during the knitting, not later. Since such a garment is shaped to the figure while in progress, you must press as you go, each time you try it on, in order to "relax" the fabric and show the true length and width so far achieved. This is especially important for garments containing lace patterns, or any other patterns that require stretching. Test swatches for such patterns must be stretched, too. Have the steam iron ready whenever you prepare to try on the developing garment. Run the iron over the wrong side of the knitting. Most solid fabrics require only a very light touch, so don't let the full weight of the iron rest on them. Lacy fabrics require a definite firm pull, both vertically and horizontally, to open up the pattern; so it will do them no harm to be pressed a little more heavily. Use the recommended iron setting for the fiber: warm for synthetics, warmer for wool, hot for cotton. Remember always to keep the iron away from ribbings, borders, neckbands, and other portions that you do not want to stretch during this process of pressing-as-you-go.

Neckbands, collars, armhole borders, buttons, and other such applications can be made just as soon as the embryo garment is ready for them. This time comes pretty soon when you are knitting from the top. Don't leave such details to the end, because the earlier the upper portions of the garment are completed, the better you can judge its correct fit. Also, when you are nearing the end of your work, it's nice to know that there won't be any odd jobs left over. In most styles, when you have bound off the last stitch, that's it. You can put on the garment, if it has been made for yourself, and wear it to tonight's dinner-party.

Pencil and paper are tools almost as necessary as needles and yarn. It's quite possible that you might want to copy your own design some day, perhaps with a different pattern stitch or slight changes in styling. To make this easy, write down row or round numbers, recording any increases, decreases, buttonholes, short rows, pattern changes, cast-ons or bind-offs that occur on each. This record may be useful in the future, but it will also be useful right now. You can use it to check such things as the even spacing of buttonholes, the exact matching of sleeve or pant-leg lengths, the correct ordering of pattern stitches, and the positioning of shaping units.

A good supply of different-colored markers will be useful also. Since the major portion of each of these designs is worked in circular knitting, you will always need at least one marker to signal the end of one round and the beginning of the next. Markers are used also, at your discretion, to set off different sections of the garment, pocket locations, pattern panels, and the positions of darts and side "seams." You can use commercial ring markers, or make your own out of little hoops of colored thread. Rubber tips for needlepoints are handy for keeping stitches from falling off the needles during the process of trying on.

Side "seams", of course, are in quotes because they really aren't there. Not one of these basic designs has any such thing as a side seam. To sew the backs and fronts of knitted garments together, as if they were cloth cut-outs, seems to me a great waste of time and of the unique qualities of knitting. The beauty of a knitted fabric lies in the fact that it is *not* woven cloth; it is an entirely different medium, with different characteristics and potentialities. It is flexible, fluid, continuous; it covers every angle and curve of the body with effortless ease; it changes position along with its wearer. To some degree at least, a seam interrupts the lithe continuity of this knitted fabric. Knitting *can* be used to make sewable cut-outs like those of a dress pattern, and is so used, more often than not. But it can also be used much more cleverly than that. A great virtue of knitting is that it can make an entire garment, following all the various surfaces of the human figure, out of one continuous thread—a remarkable feat, when you think about it. Another great virtue of knitting is that it can alter the very pattern of its fabric in different portions of the same garment, to suit different widths and angles of the figure beneath. Sewing cannot duplicate such refinements. They belong to knitting alone. Therefore, when knitting from the top, we forget about sewing and its methods of putting garments together. We do not shape our clothes the dressmaker's way nor the tailor's way, but the knitter's way—which, when intelligently handled, is unlike any other method of covering and ornamenting the human figure.

A good hand-knit may be fashion-timely, but it is also fashion-timeless. It isn't a garment that you wear for a year, and then throw away because it is out of style. It will be in style for many years, which is as it should be, considering the time and planning that go into the making of it. Furthermore, your self-designed hand-knit surpasses any high-fashion designer original in true originality. Sooner or later, thousands of copies will be made of any popular designer's style. Your garment, however, is the only one of its kind in the world. Fashion uniqueness of that magnitude cannot be bought for any amount of money; yet it costs you nothing but the price of your yarn. In this sense, you can be better dressed than the woman wearing the latest couturier style. What's more, you can have the personal satisfaction of having worked out your own ideas in your own way, meanwhile enjoying the fun of creative knitting—one of the most fascinating of parlor pastimes. Few other leisure-time activities are so richly productive of both present and future delight.

Mount Kemble Lake   B. G. W.
MORRISTOWN, NEW JERSEY

Special Note on the Illustrations

Garment diagrams shown in this book are more or less self-explanatory, but a few words might make them even clearer. Solid lines indicate cast-on, bound-off, or side edges of the knitting, as well as garment outlines and the outlines of various garment sections. Invisibly cast-on stitches, or stitches invisibly woven together, are not shown as lines because they do not reveal any demarcation in the knitting. Shaping units (increases and decreases) are indicated by dots whenever they are included in a diagram. Short-row turnings are indicated by X's. Loose stitches, which may be either on a needle or temporarily held by pieces of string, are indicated by rows of small parallel dashes.

Glossary

k—knit.

p—purl.

k1–b—knit one stitch in *back* loop.

k2 tog—knit two stitches together.

p2 tog—purl two stitches together.

ssk—slip, slip, knit: slip two stitches *knitwise,* one at a time, then insert left-hand needle point into the fronts of these two stitches, and knit them together from this position. This makes a left-slanting single decrease, like "sl 1, k1, psso" or "k2 tog–b", but a little neater-looking than either.

slip–(sl)—pass a stitch or stitches from the left needle to the right needle without working. The yarn may be held either in front or in back of the slipped stitch.

sl 1—k2 tog—psso—a double decrease, making 1 stitch out of 3. Slip one stitch, knit the next 2 together, then pass the slipped stitch over the k2–tog stitch.

sl 2—k1—p2sso—another double decrease, making the central stitch prominent. Slip two stitches as if to k2 tog, knit the next stitch, then pass the two slipped stitches *together* over the knit stitch.

yo—yarn over. Pass the yarn once over the top of the right needle before working the next stitch. A yo is usually used to make a hole.

cable cast-on—a firm cast-on used either to add more stitches at the beginning or end of a row, or to begin the knitting. In the first case, *insert the right-hand needle between the first 2 stitches on the left needle, and draw through a loop; place this loop on the left needle to make a new first stitch; repeat from *. In the second case, cast on 2 stitches in the ordinary way, then cable-cast-on

17

all the rest of them. One advantageous feature of this cast-on is that it begins at the very end of the yarn, so there are no extra strands to come out too long or too short.

mosaic pattern—a pattern made in 2 contrasting colors by using slip-stitches. Colors are worked one at a time, on alternate rows.

lace pattern—a pattern formed by yarn-over holes and decreases.

cable pattern—a pattern made by drawing groups of stitches across each other with the cable needle or double-pointed needle.

increase—to make 2 or more stitches out of 1 stitch, for widening.

decrease—to make 1 stitch out of 2 or more stitches, for narrowing.

yarn needle—a large blunt needle used for sewing with yarn.

Figure 1.
Classic Raglan Pullover

BASIC DESIGN NO. 1

Classic Raglan Pullover

We begin with this style not because it is the simplest (it isn't), but because it is the most familiar to the majority of knitters. A classic raglan is constructed in this way: first, you make a seamless rectangular yoke, by increasing 2 stitches at each corner of the rectangle every other round; then, when the rectangle is big enough to cover the shoulder area down to the underarms, you divide it up into sleeve and body sections. The short sides of the rectangle become sleeves. The long sides of the rectangle become front and back sections; these are worked together as a seamless tube all the way down to the lower edge of the garment.

The raglan pullover is worked on an assortment of circular needles. You will need a 24″, a 29″, and perhaps a 36″ needle, all in the same size, for the main portion. You will also need a 16″ and a 29″ needle a size or two smaller, for the neckband and lower border. If the garment is to be totally seamless, sleeves and all, you will also need a 16″ needle in the first size and a set of double-pointed needles in both sizes.

To start, measure the back of your neck. Average measurements are: for a child of 9 to 14 years, $4\frac{1}{2}$″ to 5″; for a woman, $5\frac{1}{2}$″ to 6″; for a man, $6\frac{1}{2}$″ to 7″. Multiply this measurement by your stitch gauge. Let's suppose that your measurement is 6″, and you are working on a gauge of 5 stitches to the inch. This means that you will cast on 30 stitches for the back of the neck (or 29, or 31, if you need an odd number to center your pattern). But don't cast on yet; some more stitches must be added.

Take one-third of the back-neck stitches, and add this many to each side for the tops of the sleeves (i.e., the short sides of the rectangle). One-third of 30 is 19

10, so you add 10 stitches (or 9, or 11, if a center stitch is wanted) to each side. The total is now 50. To this total, or any other required total, add 6 more stitches. 4 of these 6 stitches are going to be "seam" or corner stitches; they will be placed on each side of each sleeve section. The other 2 of these 6 stitches are going to be front stitches, one on each end of the row. Now you have a grand total of 56 stitches, divided as follows: 1 front, 1 seam, 10 sleeve, 1 seam, 30 back, 1 seam, 10 sleeve, 1 seam, 1 front.

Take up the 24″ needle and cast on the correct number. Do not join; for a while you must work back and forth in rows. Purl one row for the wrong side. For the next 2″ or 3″ you will be increasing 10 stitches on each right-side row, as follows: one increase in each of the first and last stitches, and a double increase in each of the seam stitches. These double increases can be worked in many different ways, so let's pause to discuss the possibilities.

PAUSE

Double increase #1: yo, k1, yo. This is a good one for any garment containing lace patterns, since it makes a neat double line of holes down the raglan seam. The "k1" between the 2 yo's is always the seam stitch; the yo's add new stitches to the garment sections.

Double increase #2: (k1, yo, k1) in the seam stitch. This increase has a handsome appearance. On subsequent right-side rows, take care that the (k1, yo, k1) is worked into the *yo* of the previous increase, so the raglan seams remain straight.

Double increase #3: (k1-b, k1) in the seam stitch, then insert left needle behind the vertical strand that runs downward from between the 2 stitches

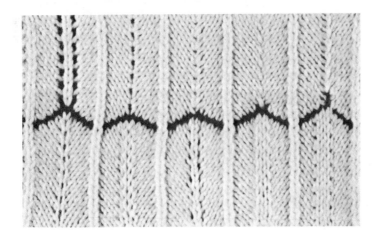

Figure 2. Double increases
ABOVE, LEFT TO RIGHT: #1, #2, #3, #4, and #5
BELOW, LEFT TO RIGHT: #6, #7, #8, #9, and #10

just made, and knit into the back of this strand for the third stitch. This makes a beautiful line of stitches fanning out from the seam stitch.

Double increase #4: knit into the back of the stitch in the row below the seam stitch (inserting needle downward into the purled head of this stitch on the wrong side), then knit into the back of the seam stitch itself, then with left needle draw up the left side loop of the same stitch in the row below, and knit into the back of this strand for the third stitch. This is the one I like best. When worked in a series, every right-side row, it makes a firm, tight raglan seam that never shows any holes.

Double increase #5: lift up the stitch in the row below the seam stitch, place it on left needle, and (k1-b, k1) into it; then knit the seam stitch itself.

Double increase #6: knit into the seam stitch, leaving it on needle; then knit into the front of the stitch in the row below; then knit into the seam stitch again. This makes tiny holes in the center of the seam stitches, with vertical bars on each side.

Double increase #7: make one (M1) each side of the seam stitch. M1 is done by lifting up the running thread between stitches, placing it on left needle, and knitting into the back of it.

Double increase #8: M1 loosely each side of the seam stitch, by simply knitting under the running thread without lifting or twisting it. This increase makes holes smaller than the yo holes in #1.

Double increase #9: make an invisible single increase in each of the 2 stitches either side of the seam stitch. The invisible single increase is: knit into the back of the stitch in the row below, then knit the stitch on needle.

Double increase. #10, or The Patriarch: (k1, k1-b) in each of the 2 stitches either side of the seam stitch. This is the oldest double increase for raglans. It's not as pretty as some of the others, but it's simple.

There are still other double increases that might be used, such as (k1, p1, k1) in the seam stitch, (k1-b, yo, k1-b) in the seam stitch, (p1, yo, p1) in the seam stitch, and so on. But these 10 are eminently suitable for raglan seams, and you can surely find one among them that appeals to you. Obviously, you can't use #9 or #10 on the very first increase row, because the front stitches are right next to the front seam stitches, and they have their own increasing to do on that row.

Double increases #1, #7, #8, #9, and #10 do not involve the seam stitch itself, so these increases can be used to make a full-fashioned seam with 2, 3, or more stitches between the increases. To do this, just steal an extra stitch or two from the body or sleeve sections and call these additional seam stitches. Very attractive raglan designs can be made with narrow pattern panels, such as small cables, in place of single seam stitches. Take the extra stitches for such a pattern from the body stitches, so that the pattern can be carried on all the way down the body of the garment after passing the underarm.

CONTINUE

Now that you have tried all these increases and chosen the one you want, and considered the possibility of a full-fashioned or patterned raglan seam, let's go back to the little crescent of knitting that is waiting on your needle. You have increased 10 stitches every right-side row until the length of the back section is somewhere between 2″ and 3″. Put the crescent of knitting around your neck and look at it. Have you come down to the level of the throat front yet? If not, knit a little more. The proper level usually is reached between the 14th and 20th rows, depending on stitch gauge and size. When you have passed the front of the throat, stop. Count the stitches on the two front sections and add them together. Count the stitches on the back section. Subtract the front stitches from the back stitches. The result is the number of stitches that you must cast on across the front of the throat, to make the front total equal to the back total. At the end of the next right-side row, cast on this number of stitches to join the two points of the crescent together, and continue knitting across the left front to the left front raglan, where you will begin the next *round*. From here on the yoke will be made with circular knitting, round and round across left sleeve, back, right sleeve, front. Keep on double-increasing at each raglan every other round, thus adding 8 new stitches to the garment with each increase round. This is the standard rate of increasing, and it will serve quite well for almost all garments. But—like all other knitting

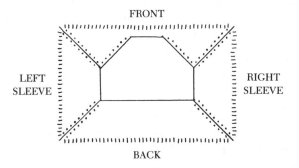

Figure 3. Top view of raglan yoke after casting on front neck stitches

rules—it is adaptable and adjustable, and you should know when and how to alter it if you have to. We'll get to that in a minute; but go ahead and use it anyway until the center portion of each sleeve is long enough to pass over the point of each shoulder. This is a convenient time to change to the 29″ needle, to accommodate the growing number of stitches; so during this change, with half of the stitches on each needle, you can spread the yoke over your shoulders and take a good look at it. The sleeves have come out to the shoulder-points, and the raglans are reaching down and outward, toward the underarm. How much farther do these raglans have to go?

While wearing the yoke, lay your tape measure along one raglan and extend the diagonal line to at least one or two inches *below* the underarm. A deep armhole is much better than a too-short one; nothing is so dismal as a sweater that binds under the arms. Most women require a total raglan length of 10″ to 11″; men require 12″ to 13″; thick-shouldered types require even more. For a young, growing child, measure and allow *plenty* of room.

Now that your tape measure shows you the number of inches still to be worked on the raglan, multiply this by your row gauge to find out how many rounds are still to be worked. Once you know this number of rounds, you also know the number of stitches that will be added to each section of the garment, because it is the same number. The standard rate of increasing adds 2 stitches to each garment section every other round; of course this is the same as one additional stitch for each additional round. So if you have, say, 30 more rounds to go, you can figure that these rounds will add 30 stitches to each garment section—as long as you use the standard rate of increasing.

PAUSE

Occasionally, though, it will be necessary to depart from the standard rate of increasing. For instance, when you are using a pattern stitch that is much more dense vertically than stockinette stitch (such as a slip-stitch pattern), a greater number of rounds will be required to reach any given length. Suppose you need 50 rounds of stockinette stitch to make the desired raglan length, but 70 rounds of your pattern stitch to make the same length. If you use the standard rate of increasing, obviously the pattern stitch will give 20 more stitches on each garment section at underarm level. Perhaps this would be too many stitches for the width you want. Therefore, when using the pattern stitch, you must space the increases farther apart in order to come out with the right number of stitches. Calculate the spacing of these increases just like any other shaping: that is, subtract the number of stitches now on one garment section from the desired number of stitches on that same section at underarm level; divide by 2 (since 2 stitches will be added with each increase round), then divide this number into the number of rounds still to be worked. This will tell you how far apart the non-standard increase rounds should be. You may be increasing every third round or every fourth round from here on, instead of every other round. There is no harm in using the standard rate of increasing as far as the point of the shoulder, because you will want to develop width more suddenly at the upper part of the raglan for a comfortable fit. After that, you can slow down the rate of increasing if your measurements tell you to.

Notice that the preceding paragraph recommends calculating the spacing of increases for each garment section separately, not for the whole garment at once. The reason for this is that you may want to increase the body and sleeve sections at different rates. Sometimes the body will call for a standard rate of increasing, while the sleeves call for a slower rate; this occurs particularly in the larger sizes. Don't let this throw you; it's easy enough to do. For example, if you have 30 rounds to go, and won't mind adding 30 stitches to each body section but want to add only 20 stitches to each sleeve section, you can increase every other round on back and front, and omit sleeve increases every third increase round. These rounds then will add only 4 new stitches to the garment: 2 single increases on each body section. You make separate calculations for separate garment sections in order to find out whether an alteration of this sort might be necessary.

CONTINUE

Bear in mind that the raglan yoke will be followed immediately by a golden opportunity for further width adjustment: the moment when stitches are cast on at the underarm. When the raglans are long enough, the yoke is finished and it is time to add some underarm stitches to both body and sleeves. If these sections already have sufficient width, you can cast on just a few underarm stitches, and decrease even these away a little lower down if you want to. If the garment sections need additional width, you can cast on more underarm stitches—as much as 3″ worth if need be. You don't have to worry about casting on too many. You can always decrease some of them away later on; a few odd decreases under the arms will never be noticed.

To arrive at the right number of stitches to cast on, let's suppose that you intend to make the back and front each 19″ wide. At 5 stitches to the inch, that means 95 stitches, or a body total of 190 all around. Perhaps there are 89 stitches on each body section at the end of the yoke, or a total of 178. You will need 12 more stitches to make the required total of 190. This means that 6 stitches will be cast on at each underarm, and there you will have the necessary total. You can mull over your stitch-count requirements while performing the next operation, which is the division of the yoke into its various parts.

End the yoke with a "wrong-side" or non-increase round. Finishing this round brings you back to the left front raglan, where you will begin working on the left sleeve. Stop here and divide up the big rectangle. With the aid of a yarn needle, slip all the stitches of the front onto a length of string; slip all the stitches of the right sleeve onto another length of string; then slip all the stitches of the back onto a third length of string. The seam stitches may be given to either body or sleeve sections, whichever seem to need them. The strings should be long enough so that their ends can be knotted together, to make sure that the stitches won't fall off. Now only the left sleeve remains on the needle. The time has come to decide what's to be done with it.

PAUSE

Do you want to make a totally seamless garment, or do you want to have seams under the sleeves? The advantage of the seamless sleeve is that it is beautiful and flexible, and satisfies the heart of the knitting purist. Its disadvantage is that you will have to work it on a set of sock needles toward the end, when it becomes too narrow for the 16″ needle. The advantage of the seamed sleeve is that it can be worked in back-and-forth knitting all the way down. Its disadvantage is that you will have to sew the seam.

If you decide on the seamless sleeve, take up the right-sized 16″ needle, and starting at the front edge of the left sleeve, cast on the number of stitches that you figured would be necessary for each underarm. This usually comes to between 1″ and 2″ worth of stitches. Cast on all of them at once, and place a marker in the middle of them. This will be the underarm marker. Then continue across the sleeve, working the next right-side row according to your pattern; remove the long yoke needle and lay it aside. Bend the 16″ needle around, join the sleeve stitches together, and continue working in rounds for about 1″.

If you decide on the seamed sleeve, take up the 24″ needle that you started with, and at the front edge of the left sleeve cast on *half* of the number of stitches that you figured would be necessary for each underarm. Then continue across the sleeve, working the next right-side row according to your pattern; remove the long yoke needle and lay it aside. Cast on the other half

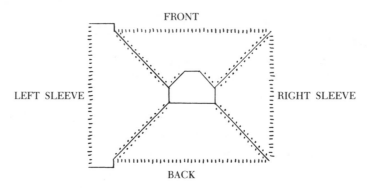

Figure 4. Top view of raglan yoke at beginning of left (seamed) sleeve

of the underarm stitches at the other end of the row. Do not join the sleeve stitches. Turn, and continue working back and forth in rows for about 1″.

CONTINUE

Having decided on the sleeve style and worked 1″ of it, you will have to do some more shaping calculation. Count the number of stitches now on the sleeve. Measure your wrist, and consult your stitch gauge to determine the number of stitches you want the sleeve to have when it gets there. Subtract the second number from the first number and divide by 2. Now consult your row gauge and find out how many rows, or rounds, it will take to get down to wrist level. Divide the first answer into the second answer to find out how many rows or rounds apart the decreases should be made. It may vary between 4 and 8; surprisingly often, it comes out to 2 decreases every 6th row or round. Leftover stitches can be decreased at the wrist, by spacing the decreases evenly just above the ribbing or border. It is better to leave extra sleeve decreases to the end, because a big sleeve is better than a tight one.

To decrease the seamless sleeve, work "k2 tog" 2 stitches to the right of the underarm marker, and "ssk" 2 stitches to the left of it. To decrease the seamed sleeve, on a right-side row, k2, ssk, work across the row to within 4 stitches of the end, k2 tog, k2. This makes a full-fashioned sleeve seam and leaves the side edge smooth and continuous, so the seam can be neatly woven.

Relax now, and work your sleeve. It will seem to go very quickly, after the long rounds of the yoke. When the seamed sleeve has grown down past the elbow, you can begin sewing the underarm seam, starting with the cast-on stitches, and bring this sewing down to within 3 or 4 inches of the needle, because a sleeve that is joined together is easier to check, when trying on, than a sleeve that is still a loose, flat piece. You can leave the sewing yarn hanging loose, ready to proceed when some more rows have been worked.

PAUSE

About sewing seams: there are several different ways to do it. Some knitters like to crochet the seams, some like to overcast or backstitch on the wrong side, some like to slip the first stitch of every row and then weave these slipped loops together, some like to work the edge stitches in garter stitch, by knitting the first stitch of every row, and then picking up the "bumps" on each side to make the seam. Most knitting teachers recommend weaving the seam from the right side, by putting the yarn needle into the center of the second stitch in from the side edge, and bringing it out through the center of the next stitch above, then repeating the process on the other side edge.

My favorite method is similar to the last one, but with a difference. I like to weave the seam from the right side, through the *edge* stitches, instead of through the second stitches from the edge. This gives an invisible seam with hardly any bulk at all. It's done like this: place the side edges together, right sides facing you, and look at them. If you have *not* slipped the first stitch of every row (and I hope you haven't), you will see that each side edge consists of a series of alternating loops and knots. Attach the yarn to the left-hand piece, thread the yarn needle, and put the needle from the right side through the first loop on the right-hand piece. Skip the knot above this loop, and bring the needle out through the second loop. Now do the same thing on the left-hand piece: put the needle from the right side into the first loop, and bring it out through the second loop. *Go back to the right-hand piece and put the needle through the *same* loop from which it emerged before, bringing it out through the next loop above. Then go back to the left-hand piece and put the needle through the *same* loop from which it emerged on that side, bringing it out through the next loop above. Repeat from *. This method attaches corresponding rows to each other very neatly, without pinning or fussing, and the finished seam can hardly be felt, let alone seen.

CONTINUE

When the sleeve is almost long enough, and its seam, if any, has been sewn about two-thirds of the way down, try it on. Are you ready to begin the cuff, ribbing, or border? How many more inches do you want to make in the cuff, ribbing, or border pattern? Hold the tape measure to your wrist and find out. Work that final decrease row for one, or both, of two reasons: to remove leftover excess sleeve stitches, or to bring the stitch count down to a correct multiple for your border pattern—whether it's ribbing, garter stitch, seed stitch, or something fancier.

Change to the smaller-sized needle (or needles, if you're working a seamless sleeve on sock needles by this time), finish the border and bind off.

For the neatest possible finish to a seamed sleeve, leave a long end of yarn after binding off, and use this yarn to start sewing the seam upward from the wrist, until it meets the sewing-strand that is on its way down from the underarm. If you have been careful about pairing the loops, or rows, as you sew, the seam should come together without a bump. Even if it doesn't, it's still better to have the bump *there* than to have a jog, showing mismatched corners, at the wrist. Fasten the sewing-strands together wherever they happen to meet, clip them to about 3", and run these 3-inch ends along the seam on the inside, one upward, the other downward.

Now your seam is tidy and your sleeve really fits. This is encouraging, and inspires you to pick up the stitches of the right sleeve from their string, and work this one the same as the left. To make sure that the two sleeves match exactly, keep a written row count during the first sleeve (circling the row numbers where decreases are made), then check off the same row numbers while the second sleeve progresses. Then there is no danger whatever of making one sleeve a couple of rows longer or shorter than the other.

When both sleeves are finished, try the garment on again. It's a funny-looking object at this point; the sleeves are completed, but the back and front stitches are flaring out on their strings. Also, the open neckline will be sagging a little. Why not firm up the neckline by making the neckband now, before going on to the rest of the body? After all, the neckline has been ready for its band ever since it was first joined together.

Take the smaller-sized 16" needle (if you have two of them), tie the yarn to the neck, and pick up one stitch from every cast-on stitch around the back and sleeves, one stitch from every row down the front slopes (or possibly, one stitch from every other row, if you'd like a tighter neckband), and one stitch from every cast-on stitch across the throat front. You know how many stitches you cast on to start; you know how many stitches you cast on across the front; and you know how many rows you worked (each side) before joining the neckline together. Add all these up, and you have the total number of neckband stitches.

As on the sleeve border, be sure the number of stitches is the correct multiple for the border pattern. If it isn't, increase or decrease somewhere as you work the first round. Work the neckband for the desired width, and bind it off *loosely*. The looseness of the final bind-off is especially important if you happen to be making the garment for a child. Children's heads are bigger, in proportion to their necks, than those of adults. Many an otherwise perfect sweater has been spoiled by a tight neck bind-off that makes it agonizingly difficult to pull over the head.

Now you are ready to finish the body. Pick up the front and back stitches from their strings onto the 29″ needle. As you hold the points of the needle in your hands, with the neck of the garment toward you, you will be facing one of the armholes. Tie the yarn to the right-hand edge of this armhole, and *pick up one stitch from each of the cast-on sleeve stitches!* This is a cute little trick that saves you the trouble of sewing the underarm seams later. (The right way to pick up stitches, of course, is like knitting without a left-hand needle; you just poke the needle through the cast-on stitch, and draw out a loop of the yarn, which is being held in back. See Basic Design #2.) If you prefer to cast on these underarm stitches for the body, instead of picking them up from the sleeve, you can do that too; but then the cast-on edges of sleeve and body underarms will have to be woven together later on. Seamless sleeves, or seamed sleeves already sewn, are right there with the correct number of available stitches, so why not use them?

Work around one body section to the other sleeve, and pick up the underarm stitches from this cast-on edge in the same way; then work around the other body section to begin the next round. Place a marker in the center of the underarm stitches, to show you where the rounds begin and end. It is helpful to place a different-colored marker in the corresponding position on the other side, in case you need it for subsequent shaping. Work even for one or two inches, then slip half of the stitches to a spare circular needle and try the garment on again.

By the way, what is this garment going to be? A sweater? A dress? A long tunic? An overblouse? An ankle-length evening gown? Is it for a man, woman, or child? I'm sure you had a pretty good idea of its ultimate purpose when you started out. But if it's a garment for yourself, you might have changed your mind by now. Let's pause to consider possibilities.

PAUSE

The average sweater—especially a sweater for a child—is worked perfectly straight from the underarm to the lower edge. In this case, you have no further shaping to do; just work your tube until it is long enough, make the lower border, and bind off. The average sweater for a man is also worked perfectly straight, but it shouldn't be. Most men like their sweaters to have plenty of room in the shoulders, but fit snugly around the hips; this feels more comfortable, and flatters their figures. So if you're making a sweater for a man, do another little shaping calculation now.

Take your man's hip measurement, allowing only an inch or two of ease. Multiply this measurement by your stitch gauge. Subtract this number from the number of stitches now on the needle. Divide this number by 2, if you want to make 2 decreases each decrease round, or by 4, if you want to make 4 decreases each decrease round. Then measure the distance from the present sweater length to the proposed lower edge, and multiply by your row gauge. Divide the first answer into the second answer, which will tell you how many rounds apart the decreases should be made. If you have decided to make 2 decreases at a time, simply k2 tog at each side on every decrease round; if you have decided to make 4 decreases at a time, work them the same as the decreases on the sleeve, 2 stitches each side of the side markers. Taper the sweater in this manner as you work downward, and almost any man is likely to praise it as the best-looking and best-fitting sweater in his wardrobe.

But suppose you want to taper the sweater the other way, in case it's for a woman whose hips are much bigger around than her chest, or in case it is to finish as a dress or long tunic, which needs a wider lower edge for ease in walking and sitting? In either case, the shaping is figured just the same, but in reverse: you start by subtracting the number of stitches now on the needle from the desired (larger) number of stitches around the lower edge; and the shaping units, of course, are increases, not decreases.

Now let's suppose that you are making a dress or a demi-fitted tunic; you want it to nip in a little at the waist, and flare out below. You will need to make two separate shaping calculations, one for decreasing, from present-garment-length to waist, the other for increasing, from waist to lower edge. For this kind of garment it is best to use 4 shaping units to each shaping round, and place them in the "dart" positions, 5 or 6 inches apart on the center

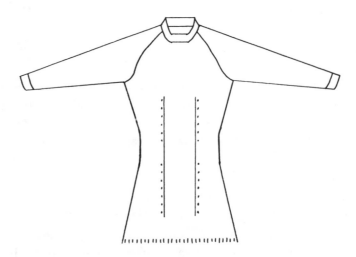

Figure 5. Shaping with dart decreases and increases

front and center back. Place 2 dart markers on the needle in the front section, and 2 more dart markers on the needle in the back section, being sure that these markers are the same number of stitches to each side of the center. Work the decreases and increases just outside of these dart markers, keeping the center panels on the same number of stitches between the markers. This way of shaping doesn't give any extra trouble, and it does cause the garment to hang better than when the shaping units are worked at the sides.

For a long dress, or a dress with a pronounced flare to the skirt, make another calculation for hip-to-hem measurement after you have worked down to hip level. In this case you may want to increase the shaping units to 6 or 8 each shaping round (1 for each dart, 1 for each side; or 1 for each dart, 2 for each side). From hip level on you will be working a seamless skirt; for additional hints, see the directions for skirts.

CONTINUE

Now that you've definitely decided what the garment is going to be, go ahead and finish it. When you think it's long enough, try it on and make sure. Work the border and bind off. There are no more seams to sew, there is no blocking to be done. It fits, because it was shaped to fit. Best of all, it is an original design, your very own. Isn't that a nice thought to fall asleep on tonight?

* VARIATIONS

REVERSIBLE BOAT NECKLINE. The simplest possible way to begin a raglan pullover is to cast on the entire neckband, all at once, instead of shaping the throat front. To do this, make a swatch of garter stitch (or any other pattern that you intend to use for the neckband), and take the gauge. Lay the tape measure loosely around your neck, placing it wherever you want the boat neckline to lie, and note the number of inches. Multiply this measurement by your stitch gauge. With a short circular needle, cast on that many stitches, and join. Work round and round in garter stitch or neckband pattern for 1″, or desired width of neckband.

When neckband is finished, divide the stitches on the needle into front, back, and two sleeve sections, having each sleeve top one-third the width of each body section, with 4 seam stitches separating the 4 sections. Proceed with the yoke, working in rounds, with double increases at the seam stitches every other round. The neck area is now completely finished, with nothing further to be done to it, and the garment will be reversible—that is, it can be worn front-to-back or back-

Figure 6. Reversible boat neckline

to-front, since both sides are alike. This is a pleasant style for dresses, light dressy sweaters, and blouses.

REVERSIBLE TURTLENECK. A turtleneck sweater can be made back-to-front reversible too, since the long collar can be folded a little more in front, a little less in back, to shape itself to the neck. Start by casting on, loosely, the outer edge of the turtleneck collar, using a 16″ circular needle and k2, p2 ribbing on a multiple of 4 stitches, or any other desired ribbing pattern. Join, and work in rounds until the turtleneck is long enough—6″ to 8″, according to taste—then divide the stitches for the yoke sections and proceed with the garment. This is a good style for a child's sweater, since the wearer can put it on either way round, and it won't wear out at the elbows as quickly as a one-sided sweater will.

REVERSIBLE WIDE-COLLARED RAGLAN. A reversible garment with a wide spreading collar can be made in the same way as the boat and turtle necklines. Lay the tape measure over the shoulders, where the outer edge of the collar will lie, and multiply this measurement by the gauge of the collar pattern. Cast on this number of stitches, join, and work in rounds toward the neck, decreasing about

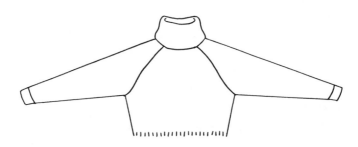

Figure 7. Reversible turtleneck

Figure 8. Reversible wide-collared raglan

10 stitches evenly spaced every third or fourth round, until the collar is the desired width and the stitch count has come down to the right number for beginning the garment yoke. Work a few rounds even, then divide up the stitches and begin the garment as in the previous examples.

V-NECK RAGLAN. To make a V-neck sweater or dress in the raglan style, start just like the classic raglan, but instead of increasing in the first and last stitches every right-side row at the front of the neck, work these increases every *other* right-side row (i.e., every fourth row). For a shallower V neck, you can increase every third row, which will mean working some of the increases on right-side rows, the rest on wrong-side rows. Continue to work in rows until there are as many stitches on the two front sections as there are on the back section, minus one stitch. Cast on this last single stitch at center front, join the work and proceed in rounds.

When working the band for a V neck, remember that you must make a double decrease at the center front every other round, to make the neckband lie flat. The best double decrease for this purpose is "sl 2—k1—p2sso" (slip 2 stitches as if to k2 tog, knit next stitch, then pass the 2 slipped stitches together over the knit stitch). Work to within 1 stitch of the center front stitch, sl 2—k1—p2sso, and continue

Figure 9. V-neck raglan

around. For a deep V with a very acute angle, these decreases may have to be made on 2 rounds out of every 3, or even every round.

SQUARE-NECK RAGLAN. This shape is easily achieved by not increasing the front edges at all, but working them straight until they have reached the desired depth, then casting on, all at once, as many stitches as are needed to make the

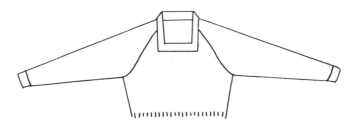

Figure 10. Square-neck raglan

front total equal the back total. The border for a square neck must have the same double decrease (sl 2—k1—p2sso) worked in each of the 2 front corners every other round.

RAISED NECKBAND. If you've found that commercial garment designs usually give neckbands that are a little too low in back for your taste, you can easily correct this by working a few short rows across the back of the neckband to raise it up. After picking up the neckband stitches, place a marker at the center back and turn short rows at 1″ intervals (or ½″ intervals, for a higher band) each side of this marker until the back neckband stitches have been worked all across. See Sleeveless Sweater (page 75) for methods of turning short rows.

ROUND-YOKE SWEATER. A rounded yoke, such as those seen in the popular Icelandic sweaters, is made just like a raglan—except that the increases are scattered, instead of being grouped together at the raglan seams. The proportion of increasing, however, is the same: four increases for each round. Therefore, if you work even for 10 rounds before increasing, then you must make 40 increases evenly spaced around the yoke; or, if you work even for 5 rounds before increasing, then you must make 20 increases evenly spaced. It doesn't matter how far apart the increase rounds are placed—this may vary, from one increase round to the next, even in the same garment—as long as this proportion is maintained. Increases are positioned *between* the increases of a preceding increase round, so that the yoke develops a smoothly rounded shape. In-pattern shaping is customary. This is not difficult to work out for yourself, if you think of the yoke as a construction of many thin isosceles triangles placed side by side, their narrow apexes toward the neck. Shape all of these triangles alike, each with its portion of the pattern. (For further remarks on in-pattern shaping, see Seamless Skirt, page 58.)

Figure 11. Round-yoke sweater

Figure 12.
Classic Raglan Cardigan

BASIC DESIGN NO. 2

Classic Raglan Cardigan

This is really another variation of the raglan pullover. It is a pullover that isn't pulled over, but pulled around instead. The shaping is the same everywhere but in front. The only other difference is that, although it may be a completely seamless garment, the body is never worked in rounds, but always in rows, going back and forth on the circular needle. Each row begins and ends at the open front edges.

However, this is a highly variable design. A cardigan is not just a sweater. It is a front-buttoned dress, or a coat, or a windbreaker, or a bedjacket, or a dressing-gown, or a bolero, or the top part of a suit—depending on its length, and the type of yarn and pattern stitch used. You can work it straight, taper it, flare it, or fit it. You can chop it short above the waist, or keep on knitting to the ankles. You can nip it in with waistline darts, as for a long suit jacket, or fluff it out with many increases, as for a wide, softly-draped bedjacket. You can fasten it with a zipper, buttons, frogs, snaps, hooks-and-eyes—or not fasten it at all. Take your choice.

Start with the usual back-of-the-neck measurement for the standard close neckline, or take the measurement farther away from the neck for a wider neckline. In either case the proportion of sleeve stitches to back stitches is the same— one-third. Work the garment just like the raglan pullover as far as the throat front, where the front bands will be started. Add up the stitches on the two front sections and subtract this number from the number of stitches on the back section, to determine how many stitches the front still needs to make it equal the back. For the sake of argument, let's assume that this happens to be 12 stitches. Now you

36

are ready to begin the front bands, and must make a long pause to consider possibilities.

PAUSE

The first possibility is a garment with a front zipper, in which case there will be no overlapping front bands at all, because the front edges will just touch over the zipper. Cast on half of the required stitches (i.e., 6) at one end of the row, and the other half at the other end, plus one more stitch at each side (making a total of 7). The two extra stitches are used to make a decorative chain edge. This is done by slipping the first stitch of every row, holding the yarn to the wrong side each time. Such an edge is tidy enough to need no extra finishing. You can also work the next 3 or 4 stitches, just inside the slipped edge stitches, in garter stitch, by knitting them on every row. This will give a firm, flat little border for the zipper attachment. Sew the zipper in by hand, and with care. Trying to machine-stitch the zipper, especially on a thick or dense knitted fabric, can lead to all kinds of lumps, wrinkles, crookednesses, and other problems.

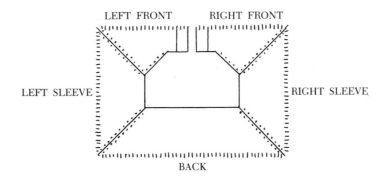

Figure 13. Top view of partial yoke for zipper-front or Chanel jacket

The second possibility is a Chanel-type jacket without fastenings, in which case there will be front bands, but they won't overlap. Cast on the required stitches half-and-half, as for the zipper, with 2 extras for the chain edges, and work the desired number of these stitches in the border pattern (read on past the end of this PAUSE for a discussion of patterns).

The third possibility is a garment with overlapping single-thickness button bands, worked in some non-curling pattern stitch. If you want the button bands

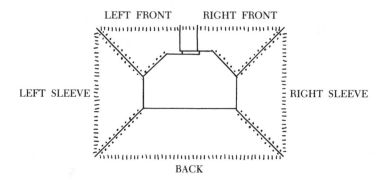

LEFT FRONT   RIGHT FRONT

LEFT SLEEVE   RIGHT SLEEVE

BACK

Figure 14. Top view of partial yoke for cardigan with overlapping front bands

to be as wide as the required number of stitches, cast on 12 stitches at one end of the row, and 12 stitches at the other, plus one more at each end for the chain edge. Then you will have the required 12-stitch width across the front; of course, when the garment is buttoned, the fabric will be doubled in thickness, one set of 12 stitches attached to the left front, the other set to the right front.

But suppose you want the front bands to be less than 12 stitches wide? If your pattern stitch gives you 6 stitches to the inch, for example, a 12-stitch band would be 2″ wide. Maybe you want it to be only 1″ wide (6 stitches). Only the *bands* should overlap; so, if you cast on 12 stitches at each side for 1″ bands instead of 2″ bands, the fronts will not overlap enough, and thus will be too wide. You would have 6 garment stitches on one side, 6 overlapping band stitches on each side, and 6 more garment stitches on the other side—a total width of 18 stitches.

Therefore, you must think of the center of each band as the center of the garment front, whatever the width of the bands may be. There should be 6 stitches to the right of that center, and 6 stitches to the left of it. For 1″ bands, then, you would cast on 3 garment stitches and 6 band stitches—a total of 9 stitches—at each end of the row, plus the extras for the chain edge. This gives the required front width of 12 stitches, for there are 3 new stitches on each side of the garment and 6 new (overlapping) stitches on each band.

The fourth possibility is a garment with double-thickness, or faced, bands. These may overlap or not, as you wish. First figure them the same as you would figure single-thickness bands, then to each side add another full set of *band* stitches to turn under for the facing, plus one more stitch for the turning ridge. So for 12-stitch bands, you would cast on 25 stitches at each end of the row—2 sets of band stitches (24), plus 1 more. For 6-stitch bands, you would cast on 16 stitches at each end of the row—2 sets of band stitches (12) and 3 garment stitches, plus 1 more. The single stitch for the turning ridge is *slipped*, with yarn in back, every right-side row, and *purled* every wrong-side row. This gives a neat outer edge that wants to turn under and stay there. The buttonholes are made double, one buttonhole being placed in the center of the band, the other buttonhole being placed in the center of the band facing, on the same row. These double buttonholes are overcast or buttonhole-stitched together when the facing is turned under.

The fifth possibility is a garment with separate front bands, which are not worked along with the rest of the knitting, but picked up later from the raw front edges and worked horizontally. In this case you may not want to cast on any new front stitches at all, because you can work any number of rows on the picked-up stitches until the front bands are wide enough to suit you. But if the present front opening is still a little too wide, and you want to add a few extra garment stitches before proceeding, go ahead and do it. Don't let the garment fronts meet, though. The bands will take care of that, later.

Now here is a digression within a digression, for this seems as good a place as any to talk about the matter of picking up stitches from a side edge. When you are making separate front bands in this manner, it is especially important to pick up the right number of stitches. If you pick up too many, the front of the garment will droop. If you pick up too few, the front of the garment will pull up short, and look very miserable.

Many knitters are panic-stricken by the prospect of picking up stitches from a side edge, and the instructions of commercial garment designs, which simply give the total number of stitches to be picked up, are not much help. In order to be sure that you don't pick up too many stitches in one spot, and too few in another, you have to divide the edge into separate inch-measurements with pins, and pick up a certain number of stitches between pins. My feeling about this is that it's too much bother; besides, I don't stick pins into a piece of knitting if I can avoid it, as a matter of principle. Furthermore, what do you do about these "total numbers" if *your* desired length is more or less than the recommended one? The recommended number of border stitches then would be wrong. There are more efficient ways to handle this problem.

When you are making a side edge from which stitches will be picked up later (or one that will be attached to another side edge), don't slip the first stitch of every row, as some knitters often do. That's only for edges that will show. Then, the side edge of your stockinette-stitch fabric will show the typical loop-and-knot arrangement—a loop every other row, the knots in between. A perfect border can be picked up on such a side edge by taking two rows out of every three. The reason for this is that the stitches of a stockinette fabric are about two-thirds as high as they are wide; so, if you were to pick up a stitch from every row, there would be one-third too many; if you were to pick up a stitch from every other row, there would be one-third too few.

Start the border, then, with the right side of the fabric facing you, raw edge upward, and attach the yarn at the right-hand corner. Work toward your left, drawing a loop of the yarn through the edge and onto the needle for each picked-up stitch. You are actually knitting without a left-hand needle. This is the right way to pick up stitches. The wrong way is to shove the bare needle through various strands along the edge. This will leave holes. *Pick up a stitch at the first loop, then a stitch at the next knot, then skip a loop; pick up a stitch at the next knot, then a stitch at the next loop, then skip a knot; repeat from *. The first row of a garter-stitch border should be *knit*

Figure 15. Picking up 2 stitches out of every 3 rows on a side edge of stockinette stitch

on the wrong side (or purled, in circular knitting, as for an all-around border), to make a ridge that will fit snugly against the edge and cover the picked-up row.

To pick up stitches from a garter-stitch fabric, such as a mosaic or some other slip-stitch pattern, remember that these stitches are proportioned differently from those of a stockinette-stitch fabric. Garter stitch is *half* as high as it is wide. Each ridge (i.e., two rows) of garter stitch equals the width of one stitch. Therefore, a perfect border can be made by picking up one stitch from each ridge, that is, one stitch every other row.

To pick up stitches from a novelty fabric that does not have either of these two standard proportions, due to an unusually tight or an unusually loose row gauge, you can work out the right proportion for yourself. It might be one stitch every third or fourth row, for a very tight fabric, or three stitches every two rows, for a very loose one. Experiment on a test swatch—it will save you from future headaches.

If the separate border is not going to be worked long enough to be turned under and form a facing for itself, but is going to be bound off along the outer edge, you should experiment with different needle sizes for binding off the test swatch, in order to get the right tension. Binding off the border too loosely will make it droop; binding it off too tightly will make it draw up. In either case, the bind-off can spoil all your careful work in getting the right number of stitches picked up. But with proper tension, a bound-off edge can make a very pretty finish to your front band.

The sixth and seventh possibilities are close relatives—a double-breasted garment, and a garment with an off-center front closure. Both are figured just

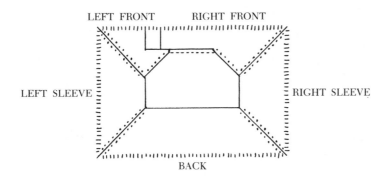

Figure 16. Top view of partial yoke for cardigan with off-center front closure (dotted line shows left front cast-on for a double-breasted garment)

like the single-thickness front bands, except that the former has two very wide overlapping pieces, and the latter has just one; the other front edge can be worked straight down. The double-breasted garment, of course, has widely-spaced double buttonholes to pick up the two buttons of the other front piece underneath.

CONTINUE

Now let's go back to the throat front, where you have cast on the right number of stitches, at each side, for the front-band style that you have in mind. You begin to work the band stitches in the pattern you have chosen for them. The pattern had better be a flat, non-curling one, especially if it's a single-thickness band. Popular fabrics for this are garter stitch, seed stitch, Three-and-One Pattern[1], Trinity Stitch[2], Daisy Stitch[3], Slip-Stitch Weave[4], and Small Quilted Cross-Stitch[5]; there are dozens of other possibilities.

Some knitters like to make single-thickness bands in ribbing, or double-thickness bands in stockinette stitch. But ribbing will lengthen, especially after buttons and buttonholes have been added to it, so that the front of the garment will droop. Stockinette stitch will lengthen also, because the buttons and button-holes will pull the band longer than the rest of the garment. To prevent such bands from pulling down your cardigan front, you must work fewer rows on them than on the garment itself. Some designers accomplish this the hard way, by knitting the front bands as narrow separate pieces, and sewing them on after they have been stretched. But there is a much easier way. Simply omit the front bands from your knitting, every 3 or 4 inches, by working short rows on the garment. Work across the row to the inner edge of the front band, turn, work back as far as the inner edge of the other front band, turn, and only then finish the row to the edge. You have put 3 rows on the garment, while putting only 1 row on each of the front bands. Even ribbing can be held to a manageable length with this little trick. Of course, if you choose a nice "shortening" pattern for your bands, like a slip-stitch pattern or garter stitch, you won't have any droop to worry about. For a very "short" pattern, such as Fabric Stitch (*A Treasury of Knitting Patterns,* p. 99), you can work short rows the other way—on the bands only.

The next thing to consider is the placement of buttonholes, if any. Knitting from the top makes buttonhole spacing easy, because the all-important buttonhole

[1,2,3]*A Treasury of Knitting Patterns,* pp. 94, 129, 153
[4,5]*A Second Treasury of Knitting Patterns,* pp. 22, 122

is the first one below the throat. The position of that one is more or less fixed; all the others can be evenly spaced after it.

You have just two alternatives to consider: whether you are going to add more neckband above the cast-on front stitches, as for a plain round neck border, or whether you are going to let the cast-on row serve as the upper edge, as for a collared neckline. If you are going to make a collar, the first buttonhole in the band will be the top buttonhole, and therefore it will be worked about $\frac{1}{2}''$ below the cast-on row. If you are going to make a plain round neck border with a buttonhole in it, the first buttonhole in the band will be placed farther down, and will become the second-from-the-top buttonhole. Let's talk about finishing up the neckline now, because you can do it now as well as any other time.

With a 24″ or 29″ circular needle, pick up the neckband stitches from the cast-on and front edges. For a plain round neckband, pick up *all* the stitches, right to the outer edges of the front bands, including 1 extra stitch at each end for the chain edge. Work the neckband to the desired width, placing the buttonhole on the halfway row. If you want the neckband to draw in a little tighter, and lie flat, make 4 evenly-spaced decreases every other row, or 8 every fourth row. Bind off firmly, not loosely; you don't have to worry about stretching a cardigan neckband over a head. For a collar, pick up stitches all around the neck but *not* from the outer half of either front band. Work outward on these stitches, slipping the first one of each row for the chain edge, and increasing one stitch just inside the chain edge, at each end of every second, third, or fourth row, depending on the desired angle of the collar points. Increasing every other row will make the collar points dip deeply forward; increasing every third row will give them a shallower angle; increasing every fourth row will make them stand out at about a 45-degree angle; not increasing at all will make them stand far out to the sides. If you want the collar to reach up a little higher in back, work a few short rows across the back of the neck to add more depth there. If you want a wide, spreading collar, work some more increases in addition to those at the front edges—about 4 to 6 increases evenly spaced every fourth row. Bind off the outside edge of the collar loosely.

If you are going to make separate front borders on picked-up stitches, collars

Figure 17. Three collar styles

should be left to the end, so that some of the first border rows can be picked up for the collar fronts. On the other hand, if you are going to make separate front borders with a plain round neckband, the neckband can be finished first, so the picked-up front border can run right up to the top of it. There is also a third, and much more elegant, way to make a final border that runs, without a break, across the lower edge of the garment, up the front, around the neck, down the other front, and so on around. This is worked last of all, as follows:

Begin the continuous border at the lower right-hand corner of the garment, after finishing the last right-side row. Pick up the border stitches up the right front to the neck, around the neckline, down the left front to the lower left-hand corner, and begin working Round 1 of the border pattern around the lower edge. Of course this is all done in rounds, with long circular needles. For comfort in handling this large number of stitches, you may need 3 or 4 circular needles; you can use them like sock needles, passing from one to the other. As you work the border, make a double increase at each of the 4 corners—upper and lower, left and right—every other round. This forms mitered corners. When the border is wide enough, you can either bind it off all the way around the outer edge, or work a purl round for a turning-ridge and start working inward, toward the wrong side, for a facing. The corners of the facing must be mitered the other way, with a double *decrease* in each of the 4 corners every other round. When the facing is the same width as the outer border, either bind it off and sew it to the wrong side, or fasten it down in the most elegant way of all, by sewing the stitches off the needle one by one, attaching them to the inside of the garment. The Picot Hem (*A Second Treasury of Knitting Patterns*, p. 342) is a very beautiful substitute for the purled turning-ridge on such a border.

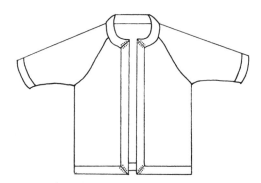

Figure 18. Final continuous border with mitered corners

But here I am talking of final continuous borders, and there you are, dear reader, still struggling past the first buttonhole and settling the question of the neckline. Having established the first buttonhole in your front band, you can make the second buttonhole a comfortable distance away from it, the third buttonhole the same distance away from that, and so on. The written row count, which I hope you are keeping faithfully, will give you all the correct distances as you progress. Whenever possible, I like to connect buttonhole rows to certain pattern rows, so that when I come to the next repeat of a particular row in the pattern, I know that it is time to make another buttonhole. This could be called accuracy-without-measuring. A very nice touch, in the case of a cable-patterned sweater or coat, is to use a diamond-shaped cable panel for the front band, and to work each buttonhole into the center of the diamond. The background stitches of this panel should be worked in garter stitch instead of purl, so they will lie flat. Many other kinds of patterns can be used in this way, too. Just think how any given pattern might look with buttons spaced vertically between the motifs.

Working the front edges straight, then, and making buttonholes as needed, you finish the yoke and sleeves the same as the raglan pullover. When you take up the body stitches again, and pick up the required number of underarm stitches from the sleeves, it is time to decide about the length and shape of the body.

PAUSE

First, let's consider the shortest style of all, a bolero jacket. This can be worked perfectly straight to the general vicinity of the wearer's lowest rib, and finished there. But it is better to taper it inward, with decreases, unless you want it to have a decided flare, in which case you would probably taper it outward, with increases. The front corners of a bolero jacket are often

Figure 19. Bolero jacket

rounded off, especially for a one-button jacket. It is best to use the final continuous border for such a garment, so the shaping can be worked with decreases at the front edges. Start about 6″ above the desired finished length; decrease one stitch on each side every third row for 2″, then every other row for 2″, then every row for 2″. Don't miter the lower front border sharply, as for a corner, but use single increases spaced an inch or two apart, shifting their positions each time you make another pair of them.

A bedjacket, too, usually ends somewhere in the area of the waist, though it may be a little shorter or a little longer. A soft, fine yarn and a lacy pattern stitch are most suitable. After finishing the yoke, you may want to make an eyelet row just below the bust (by working "yo, k2 tog" across all the stitches except a few at the front edges). A satin ribbon can be threaded through the eyelets and tied in front. After the eyelet row, increase generously—in every fifth or sixth stitch, perhaps—to make the lower part of the jacket ruffle and ripple. From this point, work in some lacy ribbing pattern or one that makes a scalloped self-border, such as good old reliable Feather and Fan Stitch (*A Treasury of Knitting Patterns*, p. 205); or apply a delicate knitted lace edging around all edges. If you work this garment all the way down to the knees, or even longer, it is no longer a bedjacket; it is a dressing-gown or peignoir.

A plain cardigan sweater is shaped—or not shaped—just like a pullover. Men's sweaters should be tapered inward, except in the case of a long (below the hip) outdoor jacket, which should be worked straight. Patch or inset pockets are useful accessories for men's garments. To make a patch pocket, make a patch and sew it on. (It sounds a little silly even to bother to say that.) To make an inset pocket, work the garment as far down as the pocket

Figure 20. Bedjacket (short) or brunch coat (long)

top. On a right-side row, work to the place where you want the pocket to be, and stop. Remove from the left-hand needle point a number of stitches sufficient for the width of the pocket, and leave these stitches on a spare needle, stitch holder, or piece of string. These stitches are destined to become the pocket lining. Turn the work to the inside and cast on the same number of stitches that you just removed, using the cable cast-on (i.e., draw each new stitch from *between* the last 2 stitches made), then turn again and continue with the row. When you have worked another 4 or 5 inches, or down to the bottom-of-the-pocket level, stop again. Take up the lining stitches on the inside, with a pair of short or double-pointed needles, and knit these stitches down to your present level, increasing 2 stitches at each end of them on the first row, and binding off these 4 extra stitches on the last 2 rows. Then, on the next garment row, knit or purl the lining stitches and the pocket stitches together, two by two (taking one stitch from each and working them together as you go across the bottom of the pocket), to attach the lining to the inside. Whip the sides of the pocket lining to the inside of the garment. If you'd rather not pause at the bottom-of-the-pocket level to wait for the lining stitches to catch up, you don't have to. Just bind off the lining stitches and sew them to the inside of the garment any time.

To make a double-thick pocket lining, work to the pocket position and stop. Take the pocket lining stitches off the left-hand needle point, and knit them into a strip *twice* as long as the desired depth of the pocket. Fold this strip in half, put the stitches back on the left-hand needle point, purl across these stitches for a turning ridge, and continue working the row as if nothing had happened. Later, you can whip the side edges of the pocket lining together

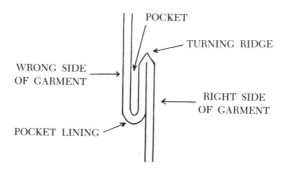

Figure 21. Side cutaway view of double-thick pocket lining (folded into position)

and either attach it to the inside of the garment or leave it hanging loose, whichever you prefer.

The jacket for a woman's suit can be worked straight if it is the short, box, or Chanel type of jacket, which does not reach below the hips. Front corners of such a jacket are often rounded off. Longer jackets should have some shaping. Use waistline darts, as for the pullover tunic, decreasing slightly above the waist, increasing below. A jacket that hangs down well below the hips should not be worked perfectly straight. This is a mistake, as it will inevitably tuck in under the seat, even on the slimmest figure, and look dreadful. Give it plenty of room around the lower edge. The widest hip measurement, plus at least 4″ more, is minimum.

The same principle applies to front-buttoned dresses and coats. A well-designed "straight" skirt or coat is not really straight; it has to have a slight flare, or it won't hang properly. As a rough general rule, any skirted garment should increase at least 1″ in circumference for every 3″ of length below the widest hip measurement. It is better to place the increases for dress and coat skirts at the dart positions, front and back, instead of—or as well as—at the sides, for the reason that a garment flared only at the sides will tend to flatten out in back after being sat on.

CONTINUE

So your cardigan grows to any length. Every now and then, try it on and ask yourself whether it's long enough yet. If you work it on a nice long circular needle (36″ or 42″) that will reach around your body, you don't have to take any of the stitches off that needle in order to try the garment on; just wear it, needle and all.

If you are making buttonholes that require extra finishing, you can finish them as you go, one by one. (One-row buttonholes usually require no extra finishing, unless they are worked double in a faced front band. See *A Second Treasury of Knitting Patterns*, p. 354.) When you are making integral button bands, you can also sew a button under each buttonhole as it is made, which helps with the trying-on and fitting. My favorite method of applying buttons to knit borders is as follows: for the right side, use a decorative button with a fairly long stem to it; for the wrong side, use a small flat button. Without making any knots in the sewing thread, but leaving about 3″ of thread end hanging out of the small button on the inside, sew the two buttons together, back to back, through the knitted fabric. Draw the last stitch through the inner button to the wrong side, cut the thread to 3″, and knot it firmly to the first 3″, which is still waiting there. Then cut off the thread-ends. The inner buttons will have knots showing at their centers, but this is a small price to pay for the extra security and protection that this kind of button application gives your knitwear. Anyway, you don't have to let anyone study your inside buttons.

If you have a faced front band, and plan to make a faced lower border to match it, do it this way. Count the number of stitches in the band facing and multiply by 2. This many rows above the desired lower edge, start decreasing 1 stitch every other row at the extreme outer edge of the facing, at the same time beginning the pattern rows for the lower border. When all the facing stitches have been decreased away, you have come to the lower edge. Purl one row on the right side for the turning ridge, and work the border facing, continuing to decrease 1 stitch every other row at the front edges as before, until the same number of stitches again have been decreased away. Then turn the band facing to the inside, and the border facing up; they will meet to form a mitered corner on the inside of the garment. Sew the stitches off the needle one by one (this makes a better finish than simply binding off); stitch the mitered corners together and tack them down. My, what a beautiful cardigan! And did you really design it all by yourself?

* VARIATIONS

V-NECK CARDIGAN. Work the V neck the same as for a pullover, by increasing at the front edges every third or fourth row instead of every other row, until there are enough stitches on the fronts to allow them to come together, allowing for the width of the border between them. Then work a separate border on picked-up stitches around both front edges and the back of the neck, or make a final continuous border around all edges. The best way to increase for a V neck is to knit the 2 edge stitches plain, then make an invisible single increase (see double increase #9) in the third stitch from the edge.

For a faced V neck, cast on the facing stitches and the front border stitches at the very beginning and work them right along with the garment, placing the increases just inside the border. When the fronts overlap enough and are ready to turn straight down, stop increasing. Work a couple of *short* short rows on half of the front border and the adjoining half of the facing, to turn the corner from diagonal to vertical. Work the back neck band the same width as the front borders and sew it to them at the shoulder.

LAPELS. If the lapels are not going to be faced, work them in a pattern that lies flat and looks the same on both sides. For a straight-topped lapel, cast on all the front stitches at once, including borders, at the beginning, and work the front edges straight down. For a rounded lapel, increase the front edges every right-side row as usual, until there are enough stitches for the fronts, including border and overlap; then continue the borders straight down in the same pattern stitch. Lapels and borders may be bound with fabric, such as satin or velvet, or given a crocheted edge.

SQUARE-NECK CARDIGAN. Work the same as a square-neck pullover, making the front edges straight until they reach the desired depth, then casting on enough stitches to each side for the fronts, including overlap. A separate continuous border works very well on a square neck; remember to work double decreases every other round at the inner corners, and double increases at the outer corners, reversing this procedure if you go on to knit a facing.

ONE-BUTTON JACKET. This is left open all the way to the waist, and fastened there with a single button; so it is essentially the same as a very long and gradual V neckline, with or without lapels. Calculate the spacing of the increases as for any other shaping. They will probably come out to something like 1 increase each side every sixth or seventh row.

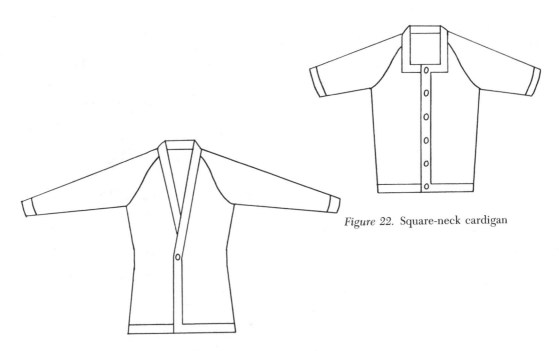

Figure 22. Square-neck cardigan

Figure 23. One-button jacket

BASIC DESIGN NO. 3

Seamless Cape

Figure 24. Seamless Cape

A cape is nothing but a raglan yoke that never ends—or, more accurately, a raglan yoke that peters out, since its increases grow farther apart and eventually disappear altogether. It is worked back and forth in rows on a long (36″) circular needle, or on two such needles if you prefer to work from one needle to the other as if you were using straight needles.

Start the neck exactly like a raglan cardigan, placing the seam stitches in the four raglan positions, and double-increasing at these positions in the usual way. The double increases are divided into two sections: the first section places them on every other row, the second section places them on every fourth row. The comparative length of each section is up to you. For a narrow, rather bell-shaped cape, you can end the first section just beyond the points of the shoulders, and carry the second section down to the elbow; from there on, work even. For a cape with more fullness, end the first section about the middle of the upper arm, and the second section about the middle of the forearm. In either case you can judge for yourself, by trying on, how the length-to-width proportions of your cape are progressing. After the second increase section is finished, work straight to fingertip length or beyond, depending on how much yarn you have or how much patience. Lower edges may be finished with fringe, scallops, an edging, or any non-curling border pattern; or, work a final continuous border all the way around.

Neckbands and front-button-bands and collars are made on a cape in exactly the same way as they are made on any cardigan. You can also make a hood by picking up stitches around the neckline, just as when starting a collar. Mark the center back and increase 1 stitch on each side of this center every other row until 51 the hood has reached the desired width; then work even until it is long enough to reach over the top of the head. Fold the piece at the center back and weave the left and right sides together at the top.

Another way to make a cape is to use a rounded shape instead of a raglan shape. This is only a matter of spacing the increases differently. Place 8 single increases evenly distributed across the cape instead of 4 double increases at the raglan seams. On the next increase row, place the 8 single increases between the positions of the previous ones, so that the growing fullness is evenly divided across the width. (See round-yoke sweater, Basic Design #1, page 34.) You can also work a cape in 8 different pattern panels, placing single increases between the panels. Or, you can use an allover pattern, either developing new pattern repeats as the stitches increase, or making the motifs larger with in-pattern increases. See Seamless Skirt (page 58).

* VARIATIONS

PONCHO. A poncho is a pullover cape, with no front opening. It can be worked raglan-style, or with a rounded yoke, just as a cape can be worked. In either case the lower edge will be straight. A more traditional poncho is made with the lower edge dipping downward at the centers of front and back, forming a shallow V shape at both points. Centered increases make the dips.

A center-dipping poncho with a reversible boat or turtle neckline is one of the simplest of all knitted garments, requiring no stitch-by-stitch directions and no measuring except the initial neck measurement. Thus such a poncho might well

Figure 25. Center-dipping poncho

serve as a beginner's first self-designed project. To do it, simply cast on the neckband stitches to a 16″ needle, join, and work in rounds to the desired depth of neckband. Then divide the stitches into 4 equal parts with markers. The markers will indicate the center front, center back, right shoulder, and left shoulder. Make double increases every other round at each of these 4 positions until the yoke has grown out to the points of the shoulders. Then stop increasing on the shoulders. Remove the 2 shoulder markers. Continue to increase at the center front and center back positions all the way down to the lower edge, changing to longer circular needles as required. After the poncho has passed elbow-level, you may increase at a slower rate if you wish, just by spacing the increases 3, 4, 5, or more rounds apart instead of 2. Finish with a border, a fringe, or a knitted edging.

PONCHO-SKIRT. A rounded-yoke poncho with a boat neckline knitted to the waist measurement can easily double as a skirt. Worked in lace, it might be a shawl-skirt; in cables or heavy textures, a poncho or après-ski skirt; in color stripes or mosaic patterns, a two-way beach cover-up. The neck-waist-band need not be elasticized; it can be secured with a cord run through eyelet holes, or else with knitted-in belt carriers which will hold either a scarf or a sash. See Seamless Skirt and Reversible Pants, pages 56 and 62.

CAPE-STYLE SHAWL. A shawl is very pretty when worked as a cape instead of in the usual square, round, or triangular shape. If you like to work lace patterns but prefer not to knit with the small needles generally used for them, you can make a very cobwebby lace shawl by combining large needles with fine yarn. Fingering yarn, baby wool, sock yarn, or thin crochet cotton can be used on size 7 or 8 needles to make an elegant cape-shawl—not for winter wear, of course, but definitely for warm-weather chic. Soft fuzzy yarns, such as mohair, also produce lovely shawls when worked on large-sized needles.

RUFFLED OR GATHERED CAPELET. This can make a pretty bedjacket or shawl when worked in lace patterns, or a short costume cape when worked in

Figure 26. Capelet

solid fabrics. Make a short raglan yoke to about 3″ below the shoulder points, then increase suddenly (1 increase every 6th or 7th stitch) to the desired fullness. The increased stitches can be worked in knit-and-purl pleats or in a scalloped or ruffly pattern stitch. Further increases can be made lower down to widen the capelet to maximum fullness before ending it around elbow level.

CAPE WITH ARM SLITS. A cape longer than fingertip length should be provided with slits for the arms to come through. Make these slits just like large vertical buttonholes, by breaking the row at the slit positions and working the back and front sections separately until the slits are long enough; then join the sections together again. Plain unfaced slits should be bordered with ribbing, garter stitch, or some other non-curling pattern. Faced slits are made by casting on extra facing stitches to each side at the top of the slit; these extra stitches are bound off at the bottom. The facing attached to the outside (toward the back) edge is turned under and tacked to the wrong side of the garment. The facing attached to the inside (toward the front) edge is not turned, but tucked into the slit and fastened to the wrong side behind the back section. Arm slits may be finished also with crochet, fabric bindings, or separate borders worked on picked-up stitches.

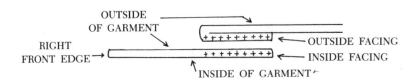

Figure 27. Top cutaway view of a faced right-hand arm slit, showing outer facing folded, inner facing straight. Crosses mark extra cast-on facing stitches

BASIC DESIGN NO. 4

Seamless Skirt

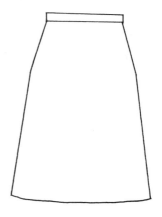

Figure 28. Seamless Skirt

The seamless skirt is a tube, wider at one end than at the other. For such a simple basic shape, it has an amazing number of potential variations in design; and when you contemplate the variety of potential pattern-stitch treatments, this number approaches infinity.

Length may vary from the short-short, or skating skirt, down through the mini, midi, maxi, and formal, or anklebone, lengths. Width may vary, in these lengths, from almost-straight to very full. The best characteristic of a seamless skirt is that it has no back or front, no right side or left side. It looks the same all around. Being knitted, it adjusts to the figure any way it happens to be put on. It will never "sit out" like a sewn skirt, because any temporary bulge caused by prolonged sitting can be whisked away, just by yanking the skirt a quarter-turn or a half-turn around the waist. Furthermore, it is comfortable to wear. The waistband is elastic and adjustable; it moves in and out as you breathe; it has no buttons to pop after dining too well, or dancing with too much abandon.

The seamless skirt is worked with 2 24″ circular needles, a smaller-sized one for the waistband and a larger-sized one for the skirt proper; also a 29″ needle in the larger size, and perhaps a 36″ needle too if the skirt is going to be fairly full.

To start, measure your waist, not too tightly. Multiply this measurement by the stitch gauge of the waistband pattern, which might be ribbing, seed stitch, garter stitch, or something fancier. Take up the small 24″ needle, and cast on approximately this number of stitches. I say approximately, because it is necessary to cast on an exact multiple for the pattern to come out right. For instance, k2, p2 ribbing requires a multiple of 4, and k3, p3 ribbing requires a multiple of 6—to give some very simple examples. Also consider, before starting the waistband, the exact multiple for the skirt pattern or pattern panels. Perhaps you will have to increase a few stitches after the waistband to achieve the right multiple for the skirt. Don't decrease for this. It is better to have several stitches too many than several stitches too few. A knitted skirt should never be tight.

Join the stitches, being careful not to twist them on the needle, and work the waistband for the desired width. Here we must pause to talk about waistbands and the various methods of finishing them.

PAUSE

There are two good ways to secure the waistband: with a ring of elastic, or with a cord. If you want to tie your waistband on with a cord, make holes for the cord to pass through, after the first 3 or 4 rounds, by working an eyelet round: "yo, k2 tog" all the way around, or, in the case of k2, p2 ribbing, "yo, k2 tog, yo, p2 tog." To make an easy knitted cord, use a pair of double-pointed needles, and cast on 3 stitches. K3, then slip the stitches to the other end of the needle, pull the yarn firmly across in back, and again k3; continue doing this, without ever turning the work, until the cord is long enough. This operation is known as Idiot's Delight. For your cord, you can use the same yarn used in the garment, or heavy knitting cotton, or ordinary string of a good size, or two or three strands of crochet cotton held together, or a combination of cotton and yarn, or macramé cord, or the nice strong nylon cord, available in hardware stores, that is known as mason's line. You can also knit a pretty 4-stitch cord with the aid of a pegged spool, or "Knitting Knobby", available in the yarn shop or 5-and-10¢ store. Or, you can make a crocheted cord. Or again, you can make a twisted cord, in the following manner: double a long strand, attach it to something, and twist it hard until it wants to kink; then remove it from its attachment, double it again, and

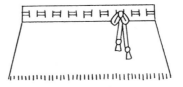

Figure 29. Waistband secured with cord run through eyelet holes

twist it in the other direction until it reaches equilibrium, and neither kinks nor untwists itself any more.

If you want to secure your waistband with elastic, buy a yard of elastic 1″ to 1½″ wide, draw it around your waist to the correct tension, and cut off the end, leaving a good overlap of at least 1″. Sew the overlapping ends firmly together. You now have a waist-sized ring of elastic. This can be inserted into a waistband casing, or attached to the back of a single-thickness waistband. To make a waistband casing, work 2 waistbands: first the inner facing, then a purled turning ridge, then the outer waistband. Insert the elastic into the waistband, turn the facing down over the elastic, and sew it in place. This method is suitable for skirts worked in fine yarn on small needles, but with coarser yarn and larger needles it becomes too bulky. In this case you would probably want a single-thickness waistband with the elastic on the back of it.

There are various ways to make a beading for attaching the elastic; one way is to crochet it. Starting at the bottom of the waistband, make a chain long enough to reach the top of the waistband about ½″ to the right. Attach the beading there, chain again to the bottom of the waistband another ½″ to the right, and so on around, zigzagging from top to bottom over the elastic. A plain herringbone-stitch is less bulky than the crocheted chain: thread the yarn needle and make a small stitch from right to left through the top of the waistband, then make another small stitch from right to left through the bottom of the waistband about ¼″ to the right, then another small stitch from right to left through the top of the waistband another ¼″ to the right, and so on around, zigzagging over the elastic. A single strand of yarn can be used for this herringbone-stitch, but yarn on the back of a waistband is subjected to a lot of wear, and may eventually break. My favorite material for this purpose is braided nylon fishline. It is very thin, adding no bulk at all; and it will never, never wear out.

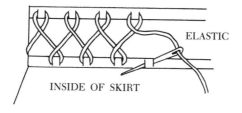

Figure 30. Securing elastic to the wrong side of a waistband with herringbone stitch

CONTINUE

With the waistband knitted and ready for its elastic or cord, and the correct multiple of stitches on the needle for the skirt pattern, you change to the larger-sized needle and start the first, or waist-to-hip, section of the skirt. Take the hip measurement at the widest point, allowing at least 3″ extra for ease. (Don't skimp. Knitted skirts look fine on *any* size hips, as long as there is enough room in the skirt.) Multiply this measurement by your pattern stitch gauge, and subtract the number of stitches now on the needle. Now you know how many stitches you will have to increase before arriving at hip level, which is probably 7″ to 9″ below your waist. Measure this distance to make sure, and multiply by your row gauge. Now you know how many rounds it will take to get there. Only one question remains: how many increases will you make per increase round?

This depends almost entirely on your pattern. If you are working a series of panels, you may have 8, 9, or 10 panels around the skirt, with a few stitches of plain purl, garter, seed, or stockinette stitch between panels. In this case you would make 8, 9, or 10 increases per increase round, one in each of the plain sections. If you are working a skirt in horizontal bands of different patterns, you can make increase rounds between bands, each time putting enough new stitches on the needle for the correct multiple of the next pattern. In this case the increase rounds need not be equal; one may have more or fewer increases than the next, depending on pattern requirements. You can arrange the number and spacing of increases in many different ways within any given rate of increasing; for instance, 8 increases every 10th round will give exactly the same taper as 4 increases every 5th round, or 12 increases every 15th round. If you want to make a sampler skirt of many different patterns and colors, perhaps to use up odds and ends of leftover yarn, you can arrange increases just as you please.

If you are working an allover pattern, the increases should be worked in pairs, one to each side of the *center* of a pattern motif, so that when new motifs are developed on the new stitches, they will match. If you have ever sewn a diagonal seam on a plaid or striped fabric, carefully matching the stripes to form neat V shapes along the seam, you know about pattern-matching. By working a double increase in the center of a pattern motif, you will automatically develop the pattern evenly on both sides. How many repeats of the pattern are contained in your multiple? Perhaps 12? Then you can work a double increase in the center of every *other* motif, to make 12 increases per increase round. Perhaps 20? Then you can work a double increase in the center of every fifth motif, to make 8 increases per increase round, or else in the center of every fourth motif, to make 10 increases per increase round. See how it works?

There is still another way to deal with an allover pattern. Instead of developing new pattern repeats on the additional stitches, you can keep the same number of motifs throughout, but make them bigger, by adding more stitches to each one. Any diamond- or chevron-shaped pattern responds beautifully to this treatment, beginning with small diamonds or chevrons at the top of the skirt and ending with large ones at the bottom. The trick is to add *two* new stitches to each motif on every increase round, to keep the pattern even; therefore the number of increases would be double the number of motifs. Since each additional pair of stitches means two additional rounds to separate the diagonal lines, and two additional rounds to bring them together again, the increase rounds automatically space themselves farther and farther apart as the skirt grows, a perfect arrangement for a graceful skirt shape. Pattern panels can be worked this way, too. All you have to ascertain, beforehand, is whether there will be a sufficient number of stitches on the skirt at hip level for an easy, loose fit. If you are working a lace pattern, you can make increase rounds very simply by omitting two of the decreases from each pattern repeat.

Having determined—or allowed your pattern to determine—the number of increases per increase round, you divide this number into the number of required increases. Then divide this into the number of rounds. Now you know how many rounds apart the increase rounds should be spaced, and you can get right to work and enjoy yourself. Any time you feel inclined, put the elastic or cord into the waistband, and try on the skirt to check its progress, first spreading out the stitches with a spare circular needle, and giving them a touch of the iron.

When you have come down to hip level, calculate the second, or hip-to-hem, shaping. The chances are that the increase rounds will not be so close together in this second section, unless you are working a full-flaring skirt. Having decided on the number of inches still to be worked for your desired length, and the number of inches wanted around the hem, you can figure the rest of the shaping in the usual way. No increase rounds are needed on the last 3″ or 4″ of the skirt, so you can figure your shaping from about that far above finished length.

One little point should be made about hem widths, to which few people have ever given any thought. A woman with narrow hips requires a greater degree of flare in a skirt than does a woman with wide hips. Why? Because both women walk with about the same length of stride. The wide-hipped woman can walk comfortably with a hem only 5 or 6 inches wider than her hips, because her skirt had a larger circumference to start with. On the other hand, the narrow-hipped woman is bound about the legs by a hem only 5 or 6 inches wider than her hips, and this pulls her skirt too tight as she walks. Therefore she needs a skirt with more flare to it, to give her room to move. Young girls, being generally narrow-hipped and also inclined to run rather than walk, are more comfortable in flaring skirts than in straightish ones.

Finish the lower edge of your skirt with a hem, picot or plain; a border of garter stitch or some other non-curling pattern; a patterned band of contrasting color; an edging; a fringe; or anything else that strikes your fancy. You can sew sleigh-bells on it if you want to. Enjoy it; it is your own unique skirt, and no one else in the world has one like it.

✳ VARIATIONS

PLEATED SKIRT. Start this with knit-and-purl ribbing, having wider knit ribs than purl ribs. There may be 10 knit stitches to 4 purl stitches, or 8 knit stitches to 5 purl stitches, or whatever you like. Figure the stitch gauge on the *unstretched* ribbing, because a pleated skirt requires much width. On the first increase round, increase in each of the purl ribs; on the next increase round, increase in each of the knit ribs; on the third, increase in the purl ribs again, and so on. The wider the ribs become, the more the purl ribs retreat and the knit ribs project. At the lower edge, bind off the knit stitches in purl, and the purl stitches in knit, to prevent excessive curling.

GATHERED SKIRT. After working the waistband, increase a lot of stitches suddenly, perhaps by increasing 1 stitch in every third or fourth stitch, for the required

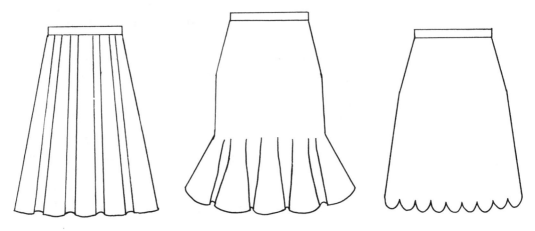

Figure 31. Pleated skirt   *Figure 32.* Trumpet-shaped or tulip skirt   *Figure 33.* Scalloped skirt

fullness. In addition, work a few more increase rounds at 4- or 5-inch intervals, this time with fewer increases, to make sure that the bottom of the skirt will continue to flare gracefully and not squeeze in toward the legs.

TRUMPET-SHAPED OR TULIP SKIRT. Work as a plain skirt, with only a slight flare, to about mid-thigh; then increase a lot of stitches suddenly and establish knit and purl ribs as for the pleated skirt. Increase each rib more and more as you approach the lower edge; bind off the same as the pleated skirt.

SCALLOPED SKIRT. Divide all the stitches around the lower edge into equal parts 3″ or 4″ wide. Work each part separately, in rows on straight needles, using garter stitch or some other non-curling pattern. For rounded scallops, decrease 1 stitch each side every other row until one-third of the stitches have been decreased away; then decrease every row until another third have disappeared; then bind off the last third. For pointed scallops, decrease 1 stitch each side every other row until only 2 or 3 stitches are left. Work these last stitches together, draw the yarn through and finish. Repeat this process on every other scallop section.

LACE OVERSKIRT. Nothing is more elegant than a skirt worked in fine yarn with lace patterns. Make it fairly full, so it will drape nicely, and *stretch* the lace without mercy when pressing. Wear it with a soft, silky underskirt of contrasting color, or simply wear it over a contrasting taffeta slip of appropriate length.

SKIRT WORKED IN ROWS. If you are averse to circular knitting, for some unaccountable reason, you can make a single-seam skirt entirely in rows, figuring it just like the seamless skirt but leaving it open in one place. Sew the seam carefully, matching pattern rows, and wear it turned to the back or side, as you wish. If you want a zipper placket in your skirt—though knitted skirts rarely require this—you can work in rows for the length of the zipper, then switch to circular knitting for the rest of the skirt. For a slit skirt, make it seamless down to the top of the slit or slits, and work in rows thereafter.

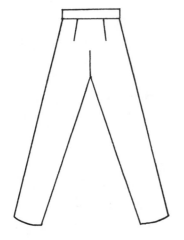

Figure 34. Reversible Pants

BASIC DESIGN NO. 5

Reversible Pants

These pants are back-to-front reversible, because that is a very good way to make pants. There is not so much difference between the back and front of the body that a flexible knitted fabric can't adjust to it; we are not dealing with a sewn fabric, which must be correctly cut and darted to fit. Naturally, reversible pants will wear twice as long as one-sided pants. Any bagginess at knees or seat, caused by wearing the pants one way, can be smoothed out by wearing them the other way. And of course, knitted pants are as supple and comfortable as a second (but warmer) skin.

Knitted pants can be undergarments or overgarments. They can be thin and lacy, like stocking tights, or soft and cosy, like longjohns, or smashingly chic, like cocktail trousers, or warmly utilitarian, like ski pants and slacks. They can have any width, from narrow to huge, or any length, from thigh-top to ankle. They can fit man, woman, or child.

You will need the same assortment of circular needles as for a skirt, plus a 16″ needle if the legs are to be seamless. Start the waistband like a skirt waistband, by measuring the waist and working the waistband to fit. If you want dropped-waist or "hip-hugger" pants, take the first measurement lower down, around the hipbones, and make the waistband to fit there. To secure such a low waistband, cord is better than elastic. If the elastic should be a little too tight, it will ride up. Alternatively, you could use a belt.

To make knitted-in belt carriers, start them on the second round of the waistband. Work to the position of the first belt carrier, then cast on to the left needle point enough stitches to reach (stretched) to the bottom of the waistband; then immediately bind these stitches off again. Use the cable cast-on. Work each belt

62

carrier the same way. On the final round of the waistband, pick up the loop at the loose end of each little chain, put it on the left needle, and knit it together with a stitch. This attaches the lower end of the belt carrier to the pants. You can firm up the low belted waistband by backing it with a loose, *un*stretched ring of elastic.

Having finished the waistband, divide up the stitches on the needle for various sections of the pants. The rounds will begin and end at the back center "seam"— which isn't a seam, and need not always be worn at the back. The first stitch of the round will be the back seam stitch. Mark its mate, exactly halfway around the needle, for the front seam stitch. Place two more markers in the centers of the intervening spaces, for the sides. The circle is now divided into four parts. Further divide each of these four parts in half with four more markers of a different color. These are the back and front dart markers, and they will be the ones you work with first.

Now establish a nice pattern panel at each side, centering it where the side markers are. You can remove these markers from the pattern panels, because the panels themselves will mark the sides. You can use narrow panels, if you wish, or wide ones that take up nearly all the stitches between the back and front dart markers, because there won't be any side shaping to speak of.

Measure the hips about 4″ or 5″ below the waist, which is where the darts will end and the crotch shaping begin. Multiply by your stitch gauge, subtract the number of stitches now on the needle, and divide by 4. This is the number of increases to be worked at each dart before it ends. Measure the vertical distance to this level, and multiply by your row gauge. This is the number of rounds to be worked before reaching the end of the darts. Divide the number of rounds by the number of increases. Now you know how many rounds apart the dart increases should be spaced, and you can begin.

For each dart increase, work an invisible single increase (see double increase #9) in the stitch on the *outside* (away-from-center) of each dart marker. When the dart increases are finished, remove the dart markers; they won't be needed again.

Now calculate the crotch shaping. Measure around the top of one thigh. Take this measurement *standing up;* when the leg is bent in sitting position, it can measure considerably less. Subtract 3″ to 4″ for the crotch stitches, which will be cast on later to begin the leg. Multiply by your stitch gauge. This is the number of stitches that will be on each leg at the end of the crotch increases. Multiply by 2 (for 2 legs), subtract the number of stitches now on the needle, and divide by 4, because you will be increasing 4 stitches in every increase round. This tells you how many crotch increase rounds there will be.

Slip the stitches of one side—right or left, whichever is handy—to a spare circular needle and try on the pants. Measure the crotch length still to be worked, from where the back seam stitch is now, through your legs, to where the front seam stitch is now. Don't pull the tape measure tight, or you will have pants that are too short in the crotch. From this measurement, subtract the same 3″ to 4″ for the crotch stitches. Then divide by 2, because you will be working both back and front at the same time. Multiply by your row gauge. This tells you how many rounds you will need to finish the crotch increases. Divide this by, the number of crotch increase rounds, which tells you how far apart the increase rounds should be spaced. It won't be very far. Space the increase rounds closer together toward the end than toward the beginning; for example, you could increase every third round for one-third of the distance, then every other round for the next third, then every round for the final third. If you got lost in the preceding calculations, you can just go ahead and do it this way, and you won't be far wrong.

Work for the required number of rounds, making double increases in, or alongside, each of the seam stitches. Use a solid, closed double increase, like #4, #5, #9, or #10. When you have finished this, each leg should have enough stitches to go around the thigh, less the final 3″ or 4″; and the back and front of the crotch seam should be within 3″ or 4″ of meeting each other. With each leg on a separate circular needle, try on the pants and make sure. If the leg stitches are coming around too far, you can cast on fewer crotch stitches; if they are not coming around far enough, you can cast on more crotch stitches. This, like the raglan underarm, is the moment for adjustments.

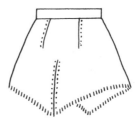

Figure 35. Pants completed down to crotch

PAUSE

For the legs of the pants, you must answer the same question as for the sleeves of the raglan: seamless, or seamed? For seamed pants, start by casting

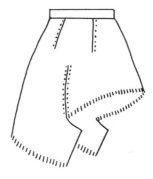

Figure 36. Seamed pants after casting on crotch stitches for first leg

on *half* of the required number of crotch stitches at *each* end of the first row, and work back and forth for 1″. For seamless pants, put the stitches of one leg on a short circular needle, cast on all the required crotch stitches at once, place the round marker in the middle of them, and work in rounds for 1″. When you are dividing the two sides from each other, give one of the seam stitches to the right leg, the other to the left leg.

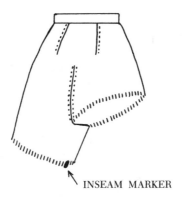

↖ INSEAM MARKER

Figure 37. Seamless pants after casting on crotch stitches for first leg

Digression for a "yarn" story, having nothing whatever to do with your present problems, except to show you that they could be worse. When I knitted my first pair of pants, I decided to make them from the bottom up, and seamless. Accordingly, I constructed two long tubes of the proper shape, and carefully wove the crotch stitches together, planning to put all the rest of the stitches on a long circular needle and have myself a good time working up to the waist with decreases. What should have been obvious—that the two legs were not semicircular, but almost completely round—was not obvious to me at the time, until I slipped them onto the long circular needle. Surprise! The circular needle immediately wiggled into a strained and painful figure-8 shape, which made knitting on it practically impossible. Somehow I struggled with it for the first 20 or 30 rounds, until the crotch seam grew wide enough to let the needle spread out a little; but it was fighting, not knitting. Moral: seamless pants should always be made from the top down. If you don't believe me, try it the other way and see.

CONTINUE

Now it is time to decide on the length and shape of the pant legs. If you want long pants tapering smoothly all the way down, take a measurement around the ankle and calculate the shaping as for a sleeve. You may make 2 decreases each decrease round, one on each side of the inseam, or 4 decreases each decrease round, with an additional one on each side of the side panel. If you want shorter pants, take the measurement at the appropriate level, calf, knee, or thigh. If you want wider pants, make the measurement as loose as you desire. If you want loose pants with perfectly straight legs, don't bother to measure at all. Just work the straight tube to the desired length.

Whether seamed or seamless, the legs should have decreases paired as for a sleeve (see raglan pullover). If you are working in rows, sew the inseam along behind you as you go, for easier trying-on. When this leg is finished, work the other one to match. Crotch stitches for the second seamless leg can be picked up from the cast-on stitches of the first; crotch stitches for the seamed leg are cast on at each side, as before. Weave the cast-on edges together, and lightly darn any loosened stitches between the crotch and the front and back center seams.

At the lower edge, you can start sewing seamed pants upward so that the upper and lower sewing strands will meet, using the end of yarn left over from binding off. Edges may be finished with ribbing, garter stitch, fancy pattern bands, or in any manner as described under Variations.

* *VARIATIONS*

TIGHTS. Use a diagonal or straight ribbing, a loose texture pattern, or, for stocking tights, a lace stitch. Simply work tight pants, by pulling the tape measure up firmly when taking measurements. Add sock feet, if desired, at the ends of the legs. Tights that will be worn under other clothing should be made of a thin yarn, so they will not be bulky.

BELL-BOTTOMS OR FLARED PANTS. To flare the lower part of the leg only, taper inward as far as the knee, then work increase rows or rounds of 4 to 6 evenly-spaced increases each, down to the desired length. To flare all the way from the hip, increase the legs instead of decreasing them, working each leg like a narrow seamless skirt. Calculate the degree of flare to the desired length like any other shaping.

CULOTTES. Make the pants fairly full, and after casting on the crotch stitches work straight down, without decreasing, to the knee. Add a fancy border or a knitted edging.

GAUCHO PANTS. Work these like culottes, but a little looser in the legs and a little longer. Finish below the knee by binding off and adding a fringe.

KNICKERS. Work these like culottes, to the knee. Measure the leg just below the knee and multiply by the gauge of the band pattern. Decrease the leg stitches sharply, by spacing the decreases close together in a small number of rows or

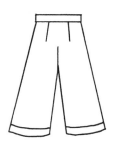

Figure 39. Culottes

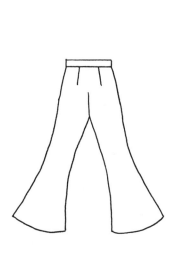

Figure 38. Bell-bottoms or
flared pants

Figure 41. Knickers

Figure 40.
Gaucho pants

rounds, until the stitch count has come down to the required number for the band. Work the band to desired width, using a non-curling pattern stitch.

HAREM PANTS. These should be very full indeed, like long pants flared from the hip, and may be worked in lacy patterns, glittering metallic yarns, and/or fancy color designs. At ankle length, decrease sharply, as for knickers, and work the ankle band. Wear lace harem pants over contrasting-colored tights or satin shorts.

SKI PANTS. Make these with sturdy yarn and a firm, dense slip-stitch pattern, so they will be warm and windproof. The legs should be slim and smoothly tapered. At the bottom, bind off all stitches except a few at the side. Keep working on these few stitches until you have a strap long enough to pass under the instep. (Fabric Stitch is an excellent pattern for straps.) Weave the strap stitches into the bound-off edge on the opposite side of the pant leg.

LONGJOHNS. These serviceable garments are much appreciated by men and children in wintertime. Knit them in nylon, cotton, or a soft wool—such as baby yarn—that will not feel scratchy on the skin. Work a deep band of ribbing around the ankle, to hold the leg firmly.

SHORTS. After casting on the crotch stitches, work each leg just a couple of inches long, decreasing rather sharply at the inseam. If you want the back to dip lower than the front, work several short rows across the back half of each leg. Finish with a narrow band of ribbing or with a border of reverse stockinette stitch (purl), which can be rolled under and hemmed to the inside.

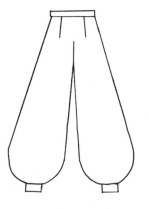

Figure 42. Harem pants

Figure 43. Shorts

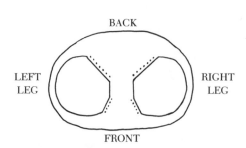

Figure 44. Bottom view of bikini or legless pants, showing lengthwise crotch shaping

UNDERPANTS. These may be short, mid-thigh, or just-above-the-knee for cold weather. Use soft, fine yarn and lacy patterns. At the lower edge, work an eyelet row and thread it with a pretty ribbon, and/or apply a knitted lace edging (see Edgings, *A Second Treasury of Knitting Patterns*). Very short underpants may have a leg casing of purl or garter stitch threaded with a narrow band of elastic, to keep the legs firmly in place.

BIKINI PANTS. Pants with no legs at all cannot be made reversible, but must be shaped to the body instead. This is accomplished quite simply by working the crotch lengthwise instead of crosswise. Start with a dropped waistline. After the sides of the pants have reached the desired length, bind off the side stitches and work the back and front separately in rows, having at least twice as many stitches on the back section as on the front section (trying on the pants will show you where the edges of front and back ought to lie). You can lower the back by working a few short rows across it, too. Continue to work the back and front crotch stitches in rows, decreasing both until each has the same number of stitches. Naturally, the back crotch piece will take longer to decrease than the front crotch piece, because it has more stitches. Calculate the spacing of decreases as for any other shaping, measuring the length to which both pieces must grow, and subtracting from each piece the last 1 inch, which will be worked straight. When the back and front meet, weave the stitches together. Try the pants on at frequent intervals to check the progress of the shaping, and you will be able to see quite precisely how it should go. Finish the leg edges with crochet, binding, or a casing—for elastic—worked on picked-up stitches.

PANTS WITH A KNITTED-IN CREASE. Work the crease stitch in the center of the front and back of each leg, by slipping it with yarn in back on right-side rows, and purling it on wrong-side rows (or slipping it every other round, in circular knitting). This is the same technique as the vertical turning-stitch used for facings.

PANTS SHAPED FRONT AND BACK. Knitted pant legs have still another definite advantage over pants sewn together with woven fabric. Knitted pants can be much more gracefully shaped to the leg by means of increases and/or decreases placed at the center front and center back of each leg, leaving the side surfaces perfectly straight. This could not be accomplished in sewing without running a seam up the front and back of each leg, an undesirable procedure. But seamless knitted pants are easily shaped at the front and back instead of at the sides. Such pants will hold a slim, elegant line when viewed from front or back, will resist bagging at the knees, and will not flop one leg against the other in walking, when the lower legs are flared. This method of shaping, therefore, is to be recommended particularly for pant suits and tailored slacks. To do it, simply place markers at the center front and center back positions of each leg, and work the shaping units on each side of these markers. Use double increases or double decreases on each shaping row or round, altering the pattern evenly on each side. You'll be surprised at the sleek, handsome fit that you can achieve by shaping pants in this manner.

BASIC DESIGN NO. 6

Sleeveless Sweater

Figure 45. Sleeveless Sweater

Of course, this doesn't have to be just a sweater. It can be a blouse, a vest, a tunic, a dress, a jumper, or the beginning of a garment with set-in sleeves. It can be buttoned down the front (see Variations), or all one piece. The point is, it's sleeveless.

To knit a sleeveless garment from the top down, we begin at the shoulder seams—only there are no shoulder seams! That is, there are no shoulder seams that you or anyone else can see, even though the garment *is* started there and worked down the back and front. The finished product has a smooth, unbroken band of knitting over each shoulder, which slopes diagonally downward from neck to arm, as a well-shaped shoulder should, yet shows no interruption of the fabric anywhere. Try to make *that* in a sewn-together garment!

You will need the usual 29″ circular needle for the body, two 24″ needles of the same size for the upper back and front (or 3 straight needles), a smaller-sized 29″ needle for the lower border, and a 16″ needle of this size for neck and armhole borders.

Start by measuring the width of your back. Don't measure too much of it; remember that the armholes will have separate borders, which will add an inch, perhaps, to each side. Allow for this by measuring only the desired garment width, less borders.

Multiply by your stitch gauge on stockinette stitch. For this demonstration, stockinette stitch will be used for the first inch or two.

Now that you know how many stitches to cast on for the back, we must make a long pause to describe that casting-on in detail. It is the invisible cast-on, which will be useful for other things besides shoulders. For instance, it is a good technique for casting on back or front neckline stitches when you want to knit up the neckband later without any extra bulk at the join. It is also good for casting on underarm stitches, for an invisible—or rather, non-existent—underarm seam. If you want to start a scarf, stole, or table mat in the middle, to balance patterns, taper matching ends, or let the length be determined by the available amount of yarn, the invisible cast-on is a must. If you want to knit a skirt from the top down, and its waistband from the bottom up—or vice versa—the invisible cast-on will do it. It knits anything in two directions without a join, and can be woven into itself or into the stitches of any upper edge. So if you haven't yet learned how to do it, you can learn now.

PAUSE

The invisible cast-on has already been excellently described by Elizabeth Zimmermann (*Knitting Without Tears,* p. 20) and by Mary Thomas (*Mary Thomas's Knitting Book,* p. 66); but I have a somewhat different approach to it, and so will describe it again in my own way. It is not only invisible, but it is unquestionably the fastest cast-on in the universe. Once you have the knack of it, you can cast on stitches as fast as you can flick your left wrist. If you started now, you could probably cast on well over 300 stitches in the time it will take you to read the following directions.

Step 1. Take a length of string, more than enough to hold comfortably all necessary stitches.

Step 2. With one needle and the end of your yarn, cast on one stitch, and place it near the needle point. Hold this needle in your right hand.

Step 3. With the same hand, hold the end of the string under, and against, the needle, so that the string passes in *front* of the ball end of the yarn. Keep hold of the string and needle together, throughout.

Step 4. Put the left hand around the long strands of both yarn and string, and keep hold of both, henceforth. Put the left thumb between yarn and string, *below* the point where the string crosses in front of the yarn. Bring the thumb forward, carrying the yarn on it.

Step 5. Put the left forefinger between yarn and string, and open it backward, carrying the string on it. You now have a diamond-shaped opening between yarn and string, with the yarn on the thumb toward you, and the string on the forefinger away from you. The other three fingers of the left hand continue to hold both strands against the palm.

Step 6. Dip the needle point down into the diamond-shaped opening and bring it up toward you, thus picking up a loop of yarn from behind onto the needle. This is the second stitch.

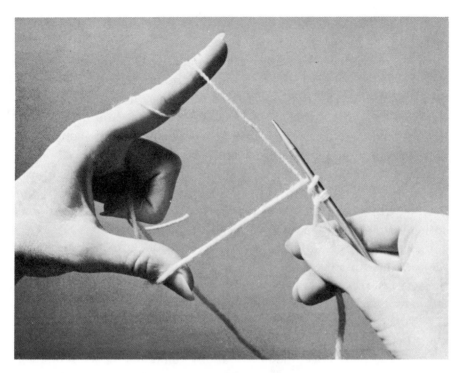

Figure 46. Invisible cast-on, Step 6

Figure 47. Invisible cast-on, Step 8

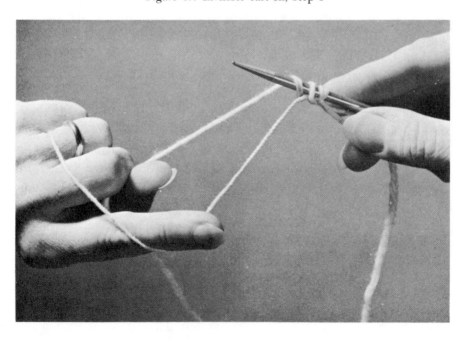

Step 7. Without changing the position of the left hand, turn it over so that the back of the hand comes toward you. This reverses the positions of yarn and string; now the yarn, on the thumb, is at the back of the diamond, and the string, on the forefinger, is at the front. As you turn the left hand over, the yarn wraps itself *under* the string beneath the needle.

Step 8. Dip the needle point down behind the yarn, on the far side of the diamond, and bring it up *through* the diamond to put another yarn loop on the needle. This is the third stitch.

Step 9. Still keeping the left hand in its position, turn it over away from you again, so that the yarn and string return to their original positions—yarn in front, string behind. As you do this, the yarn is brought forward under the string, which is still beneath the needle.

Repeat Steps 6, 7, 8, and 9 for every subsequent pair of stitches, ending the cast-on with Step 8. There will be an uneven number of stitches, because the very first stitch on the needle is an extra one. If an even number of stitches is wanted, you can work "k2 tog" at the end of *each* first row.

Now you have a lot of yarn loops over the needle, and the string running along beneath the needle with the yarn twisted around it. Be sure the string has not been passed over the needle at any point, and the loops on the needle are yarn only.

To work the first row, put the needle into the left hand, carefully holding the last cast-on loop on the needle meanwhile. Take the yarn *under* the string to the back, and begin the row, knitting all stitches through the front loops in the ordinary way. After 2 or 3 rows, you can see that the string is still holding exactly the same number of loops as the number of stitches cast on. Each of these loops will be a stitch to knit in the opposite direction. Leave the string in place until you are ready to pick up these loops onto a needle.

When you are ready to knit in the opposite direction, hold the work with right side facing, cast-on edge up. From the left, carefully slide the needle through all the loops that are on the string. Then pull out the string. Join the yarn at the right-hand edge and work the first row as follows: k1, *k1-b, k1; rep from *. The reason for knitting every even-numbered stitch through the back is that each of these stitches is twisted, and must be knitted in back to straighten it out again. If you were to knit each of the even-numbered stitches in the front loop, it would be crossed at the base, like a normal "k1-b". This might provide a *very* acute observer with a clue concerning the place where you cast on. But without such a clue, no one in the whole wide world—not even the most expert of experts—can ever see the slightest trace of this cast-on row.

CONTINUE

Using a straight needle or a 24″ circular needle, invisibly cast on the required number of stitches for the back width. Knit the first row; purl the second. On the third row, knit one-third of the stitches and place a marker; knit the next one-third and place another marker; then knit the last one-third. The two markers set off the neck stitches in the center. On the following purl row, begin shaping the shoulder slope on each side with short rows. The turnings for short rows should be made at intervals of three-quarters of an inch for the average shoulder. If your shoulders are very square, use intervals of 1 inch; if they are very sloping, use intervals of $\frac{1}{2}$ inch. Let's assume that your correct interval would be 4 stitches. Proceed as follows:

Purl across the neck stitches to 4 stitches past the second marker. Stop. Slip the next stitch with yarn in back, pass the yarn to the front, and return the slip-stitch to the left-hand needle point. Turn the work. Knit across the neck stitches to 4 stitches past the other marker, and stop. Slip the next stitch with yarn in front, pass the yarn to the back, and return the slip-stitch to the left-hand needle point. Turn the work. This completes the first short row, which has been worked to 4 stitches each side of the neck. For the next short row, purl across the neck stitches to 8 stitches past the marker. As you go by the stitch around which the extra strand was passed on the first short row, pick up that passed strand on the right side of the fabric (which will be facing away from you), put it on the left needle, and purl it together with the stitch around which it was passed. Make the turn, as before, and knit across the neck stitches to 8 stitches past the other marker. As you go by the stitch around which the extra strand was passed on the first short row, pick up that passed strand from beneath, on the right side of the fabric (which is now facing toward you), put it on the left needle, and knit it together with the stitch around which it was passed through the *back* loops. Make the turn, as before. This completes the second short row, which has been worked to 8 stitches each side of the neck. Work the third short row to 12 stitches each side of the neck, the fourth to 16 stitches each side of the neck, and so on out to the armhole edges. Work the passed strands of preceding short rows together with their stitches each time you come to them.

Of course there are other ways to turn short rows. Some people make the passed strands, and just leave them alone; others don't make them at all, but simply slip the first stitch after turning. I have described this method in detail because it is the neatest possible method for stockinette stitch, making the short rows almost as invisible as the cast-on. If you are working in garter stitch, or some fancy texture pattern, you probably wouldn't need to bother picking up the passed strands; they wouldn't be obvious anyway.

When the short rows are finished, the shoulder is shaped. Isn't that a smooth, tidy shoulder, in comparison to the awkward stepwise bind-off and bulky seam of a garment worked from the bottom up? And just wait till you see how silkily it pours itself over the shoulder when the front is worked the same way from the invisible cast-on.

Work the back perfectly straight, in rows, until it comes even with the underarm (not beyond it). Here you begin increasing to curve the back toward the front. Make an invisible single increase 2 stitches in from each side every right-side row until the back piece has widened to within 1″ to 2″ of the side underarm line. For easier trying-on and judging, you can work the front at the same time as the back if you like; you don't have to wait until the back is all the way down to the underarm before starting the front. Whenever you feel so inclined, take up another needle and turn your attention to the front.

In the manner prescribed by the invisible cast-on, take the left shoulder stitches on the needle and then pull out the left end of the string toward the center; skip the neck stitches, and take the right shoulder stitches on the same needle; then pull out the right end of the string toward the center, so that the middle part of the string still holds the neck stitches. Join the yarn at the right armhole edge and knit the first right-side row across the right shoulder; then join another ball of yarn at the left neck edge and knit the first right-side row across the left shoulder. (Don't forget to work "k1, *k1-b, k1" on this row; the left side may start with either a "k1" or a "k1-b", depending on the number of stitches it has.) This starts you off working both sides of the front at the same time, on the same needle; but you can work each side separately if you prefer. Doing both at once may make the shaping a little easier.

Work the short rows just as you worked them on the back. The only difference is that there are no neck stitches to be worked, just a gap between the shoulders. Work the fronts straight until you have passed by the fullest part of the neck (usually for about 3″), then begin to increase the neck edges toward each other. The rate at which you increase will depend on the kind of neckline you want to make.

PAUSE

A close-fitting round neckline with a plain band, or a turtle neck, can be worked like that of any sweater. Just increase until one-third of the neck stitches have been added to each side, then cast on the final third across the throat front, thus joining the two fronts together. A front slit is made in the same way, except that *half* of the required number of stitches is cast on to each side, plus extras for the chain edge if desired, and the two fronts are kept separate until the slit is long enough. Work the 3 or 4 stitches on each side of the slit in a non-curling pattern, or cast on extra stitches for facings, with the usual slipped stitch for a turning ridge. At the lower end of the slit, facing stitches are bound off and tacked to the inside of the garment, and the fronts are joined together.

A short button placket with overlapping bands is cast on just like the front of a cardigan. When the placket has reached the desired length, slip the stitches of one band onto a double-pointed needle, overlap the bands, and knit together one stitch from each band across the bottom of the placket to join them together. Collars may be added to any round-neck style.

A V, square, or low round neckline can be made by delaying the increases or the casting-on. After the first 3″, increase gradually for a V neck, working an invisible single increase 2 stitches in from each side of the neck edge every fourth row, or every sixth row for a deep V. Work straight, for a square neck, until the neck edges are long enough; then cast on all the front neck stitches at once. For a low round neck, work straight for a while, then increase each side of the neck edge every other row until two-thirds of the neck stitches have been added; then cast on the final third straight across. This is a neckline with diagonal corners, not really a round one, but when a border is added it will look quite curved.

If your garment is being made in a non-curling pattern stitch, you can get really fancy with a keyhole neck. Cast on enough stitches to overlap in the front, as for button bands, and work one inch, making a buttonhole at the half-inch mark. Then decrease one stitch every other row on each side to cut out the keyhole. When the opening is wide enough, work a few rows straight, then increase to bring the sides of the opening together again. You can finish the keyhole at the bottom with a point, like a V neck, or round it off by casting on an inch or two of center front stitches all at once. Neckline and keyhole edges can be tidied up with a touch of single crochet.

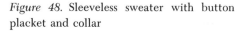

Figure 48. Sleeveless sweater with button placket and collar   *Figure 49.* Sleeveless sweater with keyhole neckline

CONTINUE

While you are working out the neck front, don't forget to start the underarm increases on the same row where they were started on the back. This is one of the occasions when your written row count comes in very handy. When the underarm increases are finished, and the back and front sections each contain *nearly* half of the desired total body stitches (less about one inch, which will be cast on at the underarm), it is time to unite back and front on the 29″ circular needle.

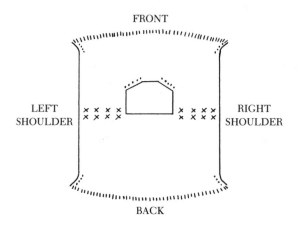

Figure 50. Top view of sleeveless sweater ready for casting on underarm stitches. (Short-row turnings are marked by X's)

(Of course if you are working an open-front style, you will continue to work in rows, all the way around the body from one front to the other.) Lay the garment over your shoulders and check its shape and length. How many underarm stitches will be needed to span the remaining distance between back and front? This is the moment for reconsideration and last-minute width adjustments. When you have figured out the number of stitches required for each underarm, cast them on, working everything onto the same circular needle. Place a round marker in the middle of one underarm, if the garment is a pullover style, and make it seamless from there on. The open-front style is seamless also, but is worked in rows on the circular needle (see above).

Now see what a wonder you have wrought: a three-dimensional piece of knitting, a garment, two shoulder-pieces and a body tube, all put together without any sewing whatever. Don't you feel clever? After working a little way down on the body, take a break and finish off the neck and armhole borders. With the 16″ needle, pick up stitches around each armhole according to the rules for picking up separate borders (see Classic Raglan Cardigan, page 39), and work the borders to the desired width. To prevent the underarm portions of the borders from jutting outward, *decrease* 2 stitches, 1 each side of the underarm line, every other round while working the border. Bind off firmly. Make the neckband or border or collar according to the neckline style. Now all you have to do is continue your blouse, sweater, dress, tunic, vest, or whatever-it-is to the desired length, shaping the body or not shaping the body to your own taste. Long, short, tapered-in, tapered-out, or straight, it is still an unusual garment displaying knitting at its most ingenious: no pieces, no seams, no patched-together look.

* VARIATIONS

WIDE-NECK BLOUSE. When placing the first two markers on the back, place them only one-quarter of the way in from each armhole edge, instead of one-third. This leaves half of the stitches in the center for the back of the neck. To make a slightly dropped neckline in back, begin by casting on shoulder stitches only, in two separate pieces; then increase one stitch at the neck edges every other row until the desired level of the back neckline is reached. Cast on the remaining back stitches all at once to join the two pieces together. For a reversible boat neckline, work the front in the same way. A wide neckline may be finished with a simple garter-stitch border, or a large spreading collar, or a lace edging, or a series of scallops (see Seamless Skirt, page 61).

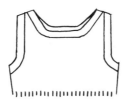

Figure 51. Wide-neck blouse with reversible boat neckline (dropped in back as well as in front)

COLLARED SQUARE NECK. A big collar is pretty when worked around the sides and back of a square neckline. After casting on the front of the square neck, work the neck front stitches in garter stitch for about 8 rows. With a 24″ circular needle, pick up collar stitches up the right side, across the back, and down the left side of the neckline. Work in rows, using a non-curling pattern, until the collar is wide enough; then bind off. For a very wide collar (2″ or more), work a few increases over the shoulders every third or fourth row.

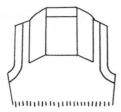

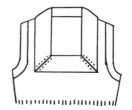

Figure 52. Square neck with partial collar   *Figure 53.* Square neck with full collar (mitered)

To make a collar all the way around a square neck, pick up one stitch from each of the cast-on stitches across the front and one stitch in each front corner, as well as the sides and back. Work in rounds, increasing 2 stitches at each front corner every other round, until the collar is wide enough. Bind off loosely.

MAN-TAILORED VEST. Make this like a narrow-shouldered, close-fitting cardigan with a long, gradual V neckline overlapping for button bands. Taper the body from the underarms to just below the waist, using 4 dart decreases. Cut away the lower front corners below the last buttonhole by decreasing 1 stitch each side every other row. Use a non-curling pattern stitch and finish all raw edges with crochet, fabric binding, narrow garter-stitch borders, or rolled borders made of reverse stockinette stitch and turned under.

Figure 54. Vest with cutaway front

JUMPER DRESS. Start with narrow shoulder pieces and a wide neck, and fit the bodice to the figure. For a belted, wide-skirted jumper, taper in toward the waist, then at the waistline increase suddenly for a full or pleated skirt. For a straight jumper, nip the waist and flare the skirt only slightly. For a low-fronted jumper, work the front neck edges straight as far as the bustline, then bring them together as for a low round neck.

BASIC DESIGN NO. 7

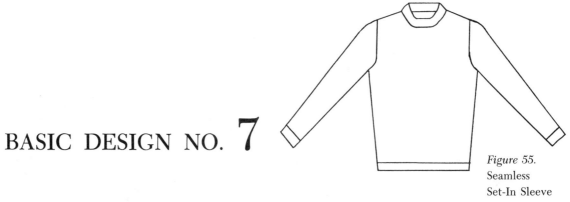

Seamless Set-In Sleeve

"A *seamless set-in* sleeve?" my friend said. "From the top down? It can't be done."

"Sure it can," I answered. "I've done it. And it not only looks better and fits better than a sewn-in sleeve, but it's easier to figure, too. Practically fool-proof."

"Well," my friend said, dubiously, "I'm sure it's never been done before."

It may have been done before, or it may not. I don't know. I have never seen it before, but then I have not seen every knitted garment in the world. Anyway, here is a seamless set-in sleeve worked from the top down, presented perhaps for the first time. It *is* a better-looking and better-fitting sleeve than the traditional one, having a very smooth cap free from irregularities. The method of working it relieves the knitter of any doubt concerning the position of the sleeve in the armhole, so that it cannot be spoiled by careless sewing or by miscalculation of the cap shaping.

To work this wonder, you will need the same assortment of needles as for a sleeveless sweater, plus a 16″ circular needle for the cap, plus a set of sock needles if the sleeve is to be seamless all the way down to the wrist. There are two ways of working this seamless set-in sleeve cap. Either way can turn into a seamless or seamed lower sleeve. I'll call these two ways the body-first method and the sleeve-first method. The body-first method sets the sleeve into a finished armhole of a sleeveless sweater, when the body underarm stitches are already cast on and joined together. The sleeve-first method sets the sleeve into an arm edge of a sleeveless sweater that has been worked only as far as the underarm on front and back, when the body underarm stitches are not yet cast on.

81

We will begin with *the body-first method.* Make a sleeveless sweater, starting with the full back measurement instead of allowing extra inches at the sides for armhole borders. After the underarm increases, cast on the underarm stitches as usual. Join the sides together, and either complete the sweater all the way down, or work just 2″ or 3″ of the lower body and then pause to make the sleeves.

Measure around the upper arm, and multiply by your stitch gauge to determine the total number of stitches that you want the sleeve to have at the underarm level. This is the number of stitches that you are going to pick up around the armhole. From this number you can subtract the number of stitches that were cast on to the body at the underarm, because the sleeve will pick up one stitch from each of these cast-on stitches to make the sleeve and body underarms match. Figure the remainder as follows. Count the rows on the side armhole edge up the back or front, from underarm to shoulder (or consult your written record to see how many rows have been worked). Half of the remaining sleeve stitches (after subtraction of the underarm) must be picked up evenly from this number of rows, on each side, front and back. It may come out to 2 stitches picked up from every 3 rows, or 1 stitch from every other row, or 4 stitches from every 5 rows, or some other proportion. Get this calculation right, and comfort yourself with the thought that it is the only calculation you will have to make.

Having decided on the proportion of stitches to rows that will distribute your desired total number of sleeve stitches evenly around the armhole, join the yarn to the body at the center of the underarm. With the 16″ needle, work around the armhole, picking up the right number of stitches all the way around. Take one stitch from each of the cast-on stitches at the underarm, and pick up stitches from the front and back rows according to your calculation. Mark the center of the sleeve, at the very tip of the shoulder. When all the required stitches are picked up, start the first right-side row, beginning at the center of the underarm. Work this first right-side row exactly two-thirds of the way around, and stop. This row will not be finished until the entire sleeve cap is completed.

Turn the work, and go back on the wrong side across the center one-third of the sleeve (which has the center marker in the middle of it). Stop again, turn the work, and make the next right-side short row across the center third to *one more stitch beyond* the place where you stopped before. Turn, work on the wrong side across the center third to *one more stitch beyond* the previous stopping-place, and turn again to the right side. Continue in this manner, working short rows back and forth across the sleeve cap and taking one more stitch from each side every time you make a turn. You will see the cap beginning to grow outward from the shoulder, while the short rows creep down the front and back armhole edges, one stitch at a time, toward the underarm. When all the picked-up stitches, except

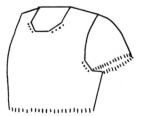

Figure 56. Seamless set-in sleeve cap in progress   *Figure 57.* Seamless set-in sleeve cap finished to underarm

those taken from the underarm, have been worked into the sleeve cap on both sides, the cap is finished. Work the final right-side row straight across the remaining underarm stitches; this actually completes right-side row #1 after its long interruption. The sleeve now has the required total number of stitches, and has grown smoothly down to underarm level without any steps, pauses, doubts, or seams!

From here on, you can make a seamless sleeve by continuing in rounds on the 16″ needle, or you can make a seamed sleeve by turning at the underarm and working back and forth in full-width rows. After a seamed sleeve has grown several inches out from the armhole, you can change to a 24″ circular needle or to a pair of straight needles if you like. If you had the foresight to leave a long end of yarn at the underarm when you started to pick up the sleeve stitches, you can use this long end to sew the seam along behind you as you work the sleeve, for easier fitting. Make the under-sleeve decreases in the usual way, whether you are working with a seam or without one.

Short rows on the sleeve cap can be turned by any method. You can slip the first stitch after turning, or make passed strands and work them with their stitches as described in the Sleeveless Sweater, or make passed strands and just leave them there. In this case the third method is to be preferred, because the passed strands will lie snugly against the armhole edges, and create a neater-looking join between sleeve and body than any kind of sewn seam could make.

In *the sleeve-first method* of making a set-in cap, you will have the front and back of the sleeveless body worked as far as the underarm, but still separated from each other at the sides, since the underarm stitches are not yet cast on and joined together. Calculate the distribution of sleeve stitches around the armhole in the same way, but begin the sleeve by casting on to the 16″ needle the number of stitches required for the underarm—all of them at once, for a seamless sleeve, or half of them, for a seamed sleeve. Then, with the right side facing, pick up all the remaining sleeve stitches around the armhole edge, and if the sleeve is to be seamed, cast on the rest of the underarm stitches at the end. The seamed sleeve begins the first short row on the *wrong* side, since you will turn and work back across the picked-up stitches for two-thirds of the distance. The seamless sleeve goes right on across the cast-on underarm stitches and begins the first short row on the right side just like the body-first method.

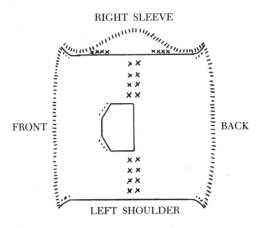

Figure 58. Sleeve-first method of making a seamless set-in sleeve: right sleeve in progress. (Short-row turnings are marked by X's)

When all of the sleeve cap has been worked except the cast-on stitches, the front and back of the body will be drawn toward each other by the sleeve, and you are ready to continue the sleeve in either rows or rounds, working across all the cast-on stitches at once. After both sleeves have been worked, and the seams, if any, sewn, you can continue the body of the sweater by picking up body underarm stitches from the sleeve underarm stitches, just as in the raglan pullover (page 29). If you have used the invisible cast-on for these underarm stitches, there is no underarm seam to be seen, and you will have a garment with set-in sleeves worked entirely without sewing of any kind. This is delightful and mysterious, and makes you feel like some manner of miracle worker, especially if you refrain from telling anyone how easy it was to do after all.

✱ *VARIATION*

SIMULTANEOUS SET-IN SLEEVE. This is a different method of making a seamless set-in sleeve, in some ways even easier than the methods given above. Here, the sleeve caps are worked simultaneously with the back and front, like the all-in-one yoke of a raglan.

Start as a sleeveless sweater, with an invisible cast-on at the shoulder and the usual short rows for shoulder shaping. Work *both* the back and front sections until the length of the piece at the arm edge is just one-third of the distance around the armhole, but *no more*. To determine this distance, measure loosely around your shoulder and underarm, where the armhole will lie. The back section should be knitted to one-sixth of this distance, and the front section to another one-sixth, so that together they go a third of the way. End both back and front sections on a wrong-side row (the *same* wrong-side row, with regard to your pattern stitch), and pause here to begin the sleeves.

With a long circular needle, work the next right-side row across the front (if the garment is a cardigan, across the *left* front). Place a marker on the needle. Then turn around the left front corner, right side still facing, and continue the row by picking up one-third of the desired number of sleeve stitches from the left side edge, all the way over to the back. Place another marker. Turn around the left back corner, right side still facing, and continue the row across the back stitches. Place a third marker. Turn around the right back corner, right side still facing, and pick up one-third of the sleeve stitches from the right side edge. Place a fourth marker. Turn around the right front corner, right side still facing. If the garment is a pullover, you will now continue in rounds, working across the front for the next round. If the garment is a cardigan, you will now finish the continuous right-side row by working across the right front to the center opening.

From here on, the back, front, and sleeves are worked in a single piece like the yoke of a raglan, but with this difference: the body sections are worked straight down, and the increases are made on the *sleeves only* until you reach the start of the underarm curve. Make 4 single increases every other row or round, one increase on the *sleeve* side of each of the 4 markers. Thus you add stitches to the sleeves, but none to the body. When you reach the underarm, however, you shape the body sections also, by increasing on *both* sides of each marker (8 increases every other row or round). This will shape the short curve at the underarm. The rest is worked exactly like a raglan yoke. Divide the sections and cast on underarm stitches in the same manner.

This is an entertainingly different way to make a seamless set-in sleeve cap. It works out very nicely and creates a comfortable, sleek sleeve without sewing. Try it.

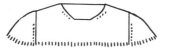

Figure 59. Simultaneous set-in sleeve in progress

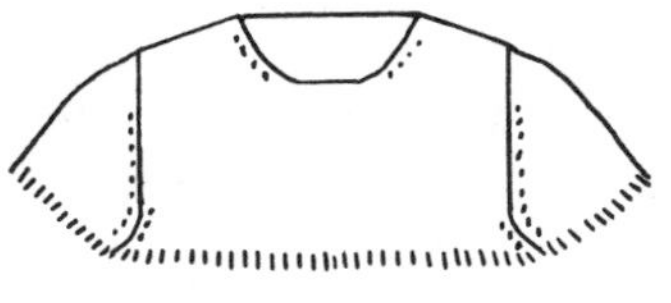

Figure 60. Simultaneous set-in sleeve finished to underarm

Figure 61.
Seamless
Saddle Shoulder

BASIC DESIGN NO. **8**

Seamless Saddle Shoulder

The saddle shoulder is a handsome, well-fitting design, especially attractive in boys' and men's sweaters. To knit it without any sewing is almost ridiculously simple once you know how to make a seamless set-in sleeve, for it is almost the same thing except that part of the sleeve cap runs on, without a break, to the neck.

Use the same assortment of needles as for a set-in sleeve. Begin by making a shoulder saddle. Cast on about 2″ of stitches (this cast-on will be the neck edge), and work back and forth in rows until this narrow strip is long enough to reach from the neck to the point of the shoulder. The saddle strip can be worked perfectly straight, or it can be slightly widened at the outer end by making single increases, 2 stitches in from each side, every inch or so. Work 2 matching strips, one for each shoulder, ending each with a right-side row. Leave the stitches of each strip on a short piece of string. If you don't mind having extra balls of yarn attached to your knitting when they are not in use, you can leave the strands unbroken, because the last right-side row of each saddle will be continued later around the armhole. Any panel pattern—a cable, for instance—with which you choose to decorate the saddle will also be continued over the shoulder and down the sleeve, without any break in the pattern rows. Panel decoration of the shoulder-and-sleeve assembly is extremely good-looking in this design, so do give thought to the possibility of using stitch-pattern interest on the saddle strips.

Now decide how many stitches are needed for the back of the garment. One-third of these stitches will be picked up from the side edge of each saddle, one-third will be cast on for the back of the neck. Lay the saddle strips with their

86

Figure 62. Saddle strips, straight and shaped

Figure 63. Beginning back of seamless saddle shoulder—top view. (Short-row turnings are indicated by X's)

cast-on edges facing each other. Join the yarn to the outer corner of the right-hand strip, and pick up the required number of stitches from the side of this strip, working toward the center. Cast on the neck stitches, then pick up the stitches of the other shoulder from the other strip. Turn and work the first (wrong-side) row of the back all the way across. These back stitches may be picked up with a contrasting color if you'd like to have the saddles and sleeves in one color, the body in another.

Proceed as for a sleeveless sweater, working short rows across the back and front shoulder sections. When you have worked down past the underarms (see Seamless Set-In Sleeve, body-first method, page 82), you are ready to make the sleeve caps. Slip the stitches of one saddle from their string to the 16″ needle, and remove the string. Continue the last right-side row of the saddle by picking up sleeve stitches all the way around the armhole. Calculate the right number of stitches to pick up as for a set-in sleeve, i.e., decide on the desired total number of sleeve stitches at the underarm point; subtract the saddle stitches and the underarm cast-on stitches; then pick up half of the remainder from the front rows,

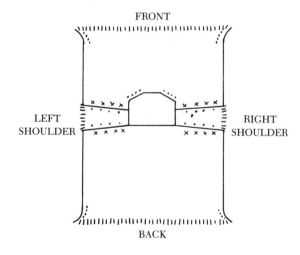

Figure 64. Top view of seamless saddle shoulder ready for casting on underarm stitches

the other half from the back rows. Divide the sleeve stitches into thirds, having the middle third exactly centered across the saddle at the top of the sleeve.

When all the sleeve stitches are picked up, continue working the first short row across the saddle stitches and down the armhole as far as the end of this middle third. Turn and work back across the middle third on the wrong side, making a second turn the same number of stitches past center as the first turn. From here on, you are simply making a seamless set-in sleeve. Form the sleeve cap with short rows, taking one more stitch from each side every time a turn is made, until you have used all the sleeve stitches except those picked up from the underarm cast-on. Then work the last row all the way around, if you are making a seamless sleeve, or all the way down to the center of the underarm, if you are going to turn there and make a seamed sleeve in rows. The pattern panel of the saddle strip—if there is one—is easily continued throughout the short-row cap shaping and is automatically centered on the sleeve, so you can carry this same panel all the way down to the wrist.

✻ *VARIATIONS*

YOKE-SADDLE SHOULDER. To start a garment with a broad saddle strip reaching all the way across the back, below the neckline, invisibly cast on *half* of the stitches required for the saddle. The cast-on row will be at the center of the back. Work even until the strip is long enough to reach from the center to the side of the neck; then cast on the other, or front, half of the strip and proceed

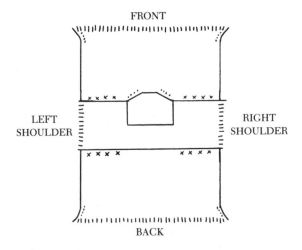

Figure 65. Top view of yoke-saddle shoulder ready for casting on underarm stitches

out to the shoulder. The other side of the yoke is started from the invisible cast-on and worked in the other direction, reversing shaping. Put the stitches on strings, as usual.

Back stitches are picked up from the entire edge of this yoke, and may be worked in yarn of a different color. Shoulder shaping can be made with short rows just below the yoke, or—if you want to do it differently—with *decreases* worked at the edges of the yoke between neck and shoulder, at the same intervals where you would ordinarily turn the short rows. This makes the yoke slightly wider in the center than at the sides, and so the back and front sections can be worked straight down without any short rows.

This yoke-and-sleeve assembly makes a very distinctive garment. The details of its construction can be strikingly pointed up with the use of contrasting colors and/or patterns, so take this opportunity to show off your pattern work to the best advantage.

SIMULTANEOUS SADDLE SHOULDER. The same all-in-one method of forming the seamless set-in sleeve can be applied equally well to the saddle shoulder. From the saddles, work the back and front until the total length at the arm edge is one-third of the distance around the armhole. Then work all the way around the piece, picking up one-third of the sleeve stitches from each side edge, *including* the saddle stitches from their strings. (See Simultaneous Set-In Sleeve, page 84.) From here on, it's all done in rounds or seamless rows, with the sleeve stitches increasing and the body stitches remaining even as far as the underarm curve. The finished garment looks like a lot of separate pieces of knitting going in different directions, sewn together with unbelievable finesse; you'll find it hard to convince people that there really isn't a seam in it anywhere.

Figure 66. Simultaneous saddle shoulder in progress

Figure 67. Back view of yoke-saddle shoulder in progress, being worked by the simultaneous method. Neckband already in place

REVERSIBLE SADDLE SHOULDER. The simplest possible saddle-shoulder design is one in which the back and front are alike, and the neckline is a plain rectangular opening. Begin by making each saddle strip as wide as the desired width of the neckline from back to front. Then close the rectangle, when picking up stitches for the body sections, by casting on straight across both back and front of the body in the same way. Such a neckline can be finished with any kind of a neckband—wide, narrow, collared, or turtle. Narrow saddles will make a crew neckline.

An even easier way to make a reversible saddle shoulder is to work the neckband first on a circular needle, then leave the back and front sections on strings and continue each saddle section from the neckband out to the point of the shoulder. In this case, back and front neckline stitches do not have to be cast on, because they are already there waiting to be picked up from their strings while the shoulder stitches are picked up from the saddles.

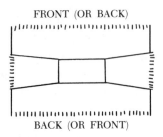

Figure 68. Top view of reversible saddle shoulder with rectangular neck opening

Figure 69. Reversible saddle shoulder being worked continuously—and seamlessly—down from a turtle neckband, by the simultaneous method

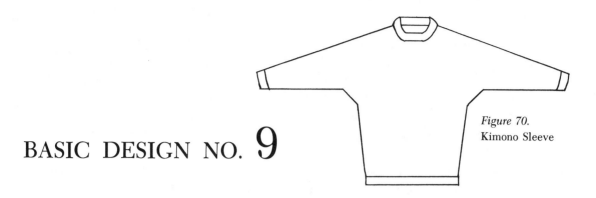

Figure 70.
Kimono Sleeve

BASIC DESIGN NO. 9

Kimono Sleeve

The kimono sleeve, worked in one piece with the body of the garment, is fun to knit from the top down—especially if you have just learned the invisible cast-on and are perishing to use it for lots and lots of stitches. The finished kimono sleeve displays a marvel of technical virtuosity: it is worked *around* the arm instead of along it, yet shows no joins and is apparently perfectly seamless. Of course this marvel is very simply achieved by using the invisible cast-on at the outer edges of the sleeve, and the ordinary weaving or Kitchener stitch (which is commonly used to finish the toes of socks) at the inner edges.

For an open-front cardigan style, you will need a long (36″) circular needle, which will serve for the entire garment except borders. For a pullover style, you will also need a 29″ circular needle. Sleeve borders, if separate, will require a set of double-pointed needles in a smaller size for narrow sleeves, or a 16″ circular needle for wide sleeves, or straight needles if the sleeve borders are to be added before the sleeves are closed at the bottom.

To start, measure the back of your neck and multiply by the stitch gauge. Then measure from the side of the neck over one shoulder and down the arm to the desired sleeve length. Multiply this measurement by 2 (for 2 shoulders), and then by the stitch gauge. Add the neck stitches to this total. With the long circular needle and a long piece of string, invisibly cast on this many stitches for the entire back. If you want to work the sleeve borders at the same time as the rest of the sleeves, cast on sleeve border stitches too, at each end, and work these stitches in a non-curling pattern just as you work an integral button band on the front of a cardigan.

91

Work in rows, as for the back of a sleeveless sweater, placing markers on each side of the neck stitches and then working short-row shaping with turns about 1″ apart. If the sleeves are longer than elbow length, there will be a good many short rows before you finally work the last row all the way across from one sleeve edge to the other. If you have border stitches on the needle, these stitches are not included in the short-row shaping.

After the short rows are finished, measure around your arm at sleeve-edge level, as usual allowing for ease. Divide by 2 and multiply by your row gauge. This will be the number of rows still to be worked across the back until you have spanned the length from upper to lower sleeve "seams". On the last one of these rows, you must place 2 markers to divide sleeve stitches from body stitches. Determine the number of body stitches by taking half of the total chest circumference of the garment and multiplying by the stitch gauge. Subtract this number from the number of stitches now on the needle, and divide by 2. This gives the number of sleeve stitches on each side. Work this many sleeve stitches, place a marker, work the body stitches, place another marker, and work the remaining sleeve stitches. Leave all back stitches on a length of string or an extra 36″ needle.

To start the front, take up the invisibly cast-on stitches of the left sleeve, skip the neck stitches, and take up the invisibly cast-on stitches of the right sleeve onto the same needle. Join the yarn at the right sleeve edge and work the first row of the right sleeve, then join another ball of yarn at the left neck edge and work the first row of the left sleeve. Working both sides at the same time, on the same needle, will help you to match rows and shaping; but if you prefer to work the fronts separately, you can start with just one of the sleeves. (See Sleeveless Sweater, page 76.) Work the front short rows the same as the back short rows, reversing shaping. When the neck edge has reached a length of about 3″, or enough to pass the broad part of the neck, begin working single increases every other row at the neck edges to make them curve toward each other. When this curve has added about one-third of the neck stitches to each side, cast on the remaining neck stitches straight across the front to make the back total equal to the front total. This joins the fronts together at the throat, like the raglan pullover, although you still continue to work in long rows from one sleeve edge to the other, and do not start circular knitting until the sleeves are finished. For an open-front cardigan style, of course you don't join the fronts at all, but simply cast on the required number of stitches for front bands to each side in the ordinary way.

Finish the sleeve fronts to the same length as the sleeve backs, and on the last row place the body markers the same number of stitches in from each side edge. At this point, the garment is a loose rectangle that is tried on simply by laying it over the shoulders to see if it hangs low enough under the arm for a comfortably roomy sleeve. If it does, you are ready to put the sleeves together.

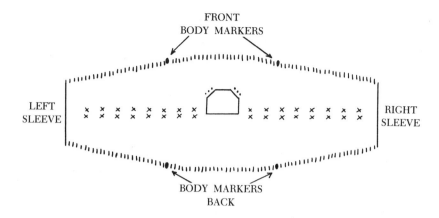

Figure 71. Top view of kimono-sleeve yoke ready for weaving sleeve stitches. (Short-row turnings are indicated by X's)

You can make sleeve borders now, by picking up border stitches from the arm edges before they are joined at the bottom, and working the border in rows; or, you can make seamless separate borders later, by picking up border stitches around the joined sleeve with double-pointed needles. If the borders have been worked along with the sleeves, they are woven together with all the rest of the under-sleeve seams.

Invisible under-sleeve seams are made by weaving the stitches with a yarn needle (Kitchener stitch). Begin at the outer edge of each sleeve, and stop 2″ *before* the body markers, so that 2″ of sleeve stitches remain unwoven on each side. Put all stitches on one circular needle to work the seamless body. The unwoven sleeve stitches now form underarm gussets, which will be tapered down into the body in one of two ways: (1) work a single decrease every other row (for a cardigan) or round (for a pullover) on the *sleeve* side of each of the four markers; or (2) work a double decrease every other row or round in the center of each gusset, between the markers. To make a single central stitch dividing front from back, so that you can work double decreases like sl 1—k2 tog—psso, or sl 2—k1—p2sso, cast on *one* stitch at each underarm during the first body row or round. To achieve the best results with single decreases, work them in pairs as on an ordinary sleeve: k2 tog at one side of each gusset, ssk at the other side.

Continue to decrease the remaining sleeve stitches, in either of these two ways, until all of them have been eliminated and the garment is left with the correct width for the rest of the body. Remove the markers. The sleeves are now joined to the body with ease and flexibility; inside each gusset there is plenty of room under the arm. A small hole will be left beneath each sleeve where the woven stitches meet the knitted stitches. Lightly darn these small holes to close them up, using the yarn-ends left over from weaving the sleeves.

Figure 72. Batwing sleeves

PAUSE

Deep dolman or batwing sleeves can be made by working long gussets. Weave the sleeve stitches together only as far in as the elbow, leaving all the rest of the sleeve stitches to be decreased gradually into the body. The underarm curvature depends entirely upon how far out from the body markers you stop weaving the sleeves. A short curve is created by bringing the weaving in to only an inch or so from the markers; a longer curve is created by stopping 2″, 3″, or 4″ away from the markers.

You can also make a dolman sleeve by working short rows at the bottom of the sleeve as well as at the top. Make these just like shoulder short rows, with the first turns about 1″ *outside* of each body marker, and subsequent turns at 1″ intervals beyond. Work a final row across, then weave the sleeves together.

CONTINUE

Having finished the kimono sleeves, work the rest of the body like any other garment, with shaping or not-shaping, ending at bolero, sweater, or jacket length, or continuing to dress or coat length. If you have not yet worked the sleeve borders, you can do it any time now, picking up stitches around the sleeves with sock needles (for a narrow sleeve) or a 16″ needle (for a wide sleeve). Finish the neckband or collar, too, unless you are planning to make a final continuous border as described under the raglan cardigan. Sew buttons under the buttonholes if you have been making buttonholes. When the garment is completed, you can puzzle your friends with those smooth, sophisticated, around-the-arm sleeves, shaped in the knitter's way without any obvious interruption in the knitting.

* VARIATIONS

KIMONO SLEEVE FINISHED WITH FRINGE. Instead of weaving the under-sleeve stitches together, you can tie them together with the fringe strands, leaving the long ends hanging down. Or, bind off the under-sleeve stitches together, as follows: slip 1 stitch from the front and back alternately onto the same needle, until all stitches that are to be fastened together are on the needle; then bind off on the right side, working "k2 tog" each time you bind off. This will fasten the fronts and backs of the sleeves in a firm join, leaving a little welt on the outside. Thread the fringe strands into each bound-off stitch along this welt.

BABY CLOTHES. The kimono sleeve is a good design for a baby jacket. Small babies' garments can be knitted without any short-row shaping at all; straight-topped sleeves worked in one piece with the body will fit very well. A long coat for a little baby can be knitted perfectly straight all the way down, with kimono sleeves attached to the upper corners of its rectangular outline. To make it fancy, finish it off with a pretty lace edging.

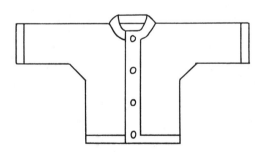

Figure 73. Baby jacket with unshaped kimono sleeves

KIMONO-SLEEVE KIMONO. To make the traditional wide sleeve, work the top of the sleeve without shaping, or shape it lightly with just a few short rows, turned at fairly wide intervals. Increase the front edges gradually from neck to waist, in a long, diagonal, overlapping V, calculating the rate of increase as for any other shaping, so that the increases end just above the waist on each side. This is like a double-breasted garment, except that the increasing ends below the bust instead of above it. Add a continuous border around front and neck edges. Fasten the

Figure 74. Kimono-sleeve kimono

kimono with a button on either side of the waist, or with a sash in the traditional style.

SADDLE KIMONO. Hybrid saddle-kimono sleeves can be made very simply by starting from saddle strips instead of from an invisible cast-on. Make each saddle strip long enough to reach from the neck over the shoulder to the lower edge of the sleeve. Then pick up stitches for the front and back from these strips, just as in the seamless saddle shoulder, and continue the kimono-style garment. Contrasting color used in the saddle strips will make a "racing stripe" effect; or, contrasting pattern panels can be run down the sleeves on these strips. Combination of the elements of two basic design styles to create a third one usually leads to attractive possibilities for interesting and unique garments.

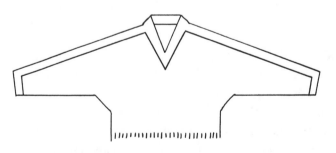

Figure 75. Saddle kimono

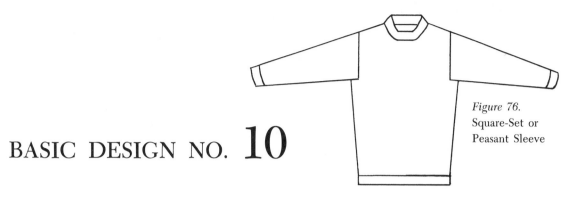

Figure 76.
Square-Set or
Peasant Sleeve

BASIC DESIGN NO. 10

Square-Set or Peasant Sleeve

This beautiful sleeve style has been unjustly neglected by many designers, perhaps because it is not as familiar as other styles. Certainly it cannot be overlooked because of any inherent technical difficulty, because it is one of the easiest of all to knit. It involves practically no shaping whatever. Both the top of the sleeve and the adjoining side of the garment are perfectly straight lines, without increases, decreases, or short rows. This simplicity of line lends itself to a multitude of different pattern treatments and delightful touches of decoration.

This from-the-top version is worked back and forth in rows for about two-thirds of the garment, yet the finished product has no seams except the under-sleeve seams—and even those can be eliminated, if you wish. You will need two 29″ circular needles, a larger one for the garment, a smaller one for the border. You may use straight needles for the yoke and sleeves, but working back and forth on a 29″ needle will serve just as well. The neckband will require a 16″ circular needle, and the sleeves, if seamless, will require a set of sock needles for the cuffs.

Begin just like a sleeveless sweater, taking the first measurement from the full width of the back. Make short rows on the back and front shoulder sections, as usual, then work straight down, without any underarm shaping, to about 2″ or 3″ below the underarm. Leave the back and front stitches on strings. The yoke is now a rectangle, with a hole in the middle of it for the neck. From the side edges of this rectangle you will pick up stitches for the sleeves.

Decide how many stitches will be necessary for the widest part of the sleeve, by measuring very loosely around the upper arm and multiplying by your stitch gauge. Pick up this number of stitches from one side edge of the rectangle—half   97

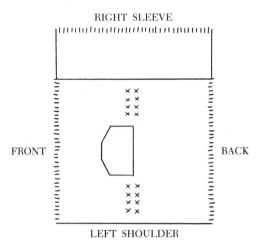

Figure 77. Top view of square-set sleeve yoke, with right sleeve in progress

of them from the back, the other half from the front. On the first row after picking up the stitches, cast on one more stitch at each end. These 2 extra stitches will disappear, later, when the body underarm stitches are picked up just inside of them.

Work even, without any shaping, until the sleeve is at least 4″ or 5″ long. Try on the yoke (by sticking your head through the neck hole) in order to contemplate the future fit of the sleeve. Pinch the side edges of the sleeve together under the arm, at a comfortable distance away from the body. Count the number of rows on the sleeve between the body and the pinch, and put a little piece of contrasting-colored yarn through the knitting on both sides of the sleeve at the pinch point. That's where the bottom of the sleeve will open out backward and forward, forming its right-angled inset. The rest of the sleeve, of course, will be seamed.

PAUSE

If you want to make a seamless sleeve, you can bring the sleeve stitches together on a 16″ circular needle at the point where they will be joined. But the sleeves must be worked in rows before reaching that point. The first few inches are left open to accommodate additional body stitches. Remember that the body rectangle is still only as wide as the shoulders, and it is going to need more stitches at each underarm to reach all the way around. If you were to start working a seamless sleeve as soon as the sleeve stitches were picked up, there would be no room for extra body stitches, and the garment would be impossibly tight.

CONTINUE

Calculate the shaping of the sleeve from its present length to the wrist, and decrease accordingly. After the sleeve is bound off, leave a long end of yarn and use it to start sewing the sleeve seam up toward the body. Don't sew this seam all the way. Sew it only as far as the marked pinch point. Work the other sleeve to match.

When both sleeves are finished, place the back and front sections on the 29″ circular needle. Now you will add the extra body stitches cleverly by picking them up from the open side edges of the sleeves, and will continue working the seamless lower portion of the body. Measure the width of the front and back sections and decide how many inches of stitches you will need at each underarm to make the desired total. Spread open the sleeve and see if the required number of underarm stitches will fit nicely across its side edges, half of the stitches to each side of the seam. Here you can make adjustments if necessary. If the sleeve opens up too much, sew the seam a little bit higher. If the sleeve opening is too narrow, unpick a little bit of the seam. When the sleeve opening is arranged to suit you, pick up the body stitches across it, work around to the other sleeve, and do the same thing there. Go on across the other body section, and continue working in rounds. After the underarm stitches are picked up, the yoke-and-sleeve construction is finished, and the rest is just the usual shaped or unshaped tube.

In case you prefer to make the entire body first, and the sleeves later, you can do it that way too. Having arrived at the proper level below the underarm, work the first round of the lower body by casting on the required number of stitches straight across each underarm opening, thus joining the front and back sections together, and continue on down the body. To begin a sleeve, pick up the sleeve stitches around the back and front side edges, but do not pick up any stitches from the underarm cast-on. You don't need to cast on the 2 extra stitches on the first sleeve row, either. As you finish each row of the sleeve, work the final stitch of the row together with an underarm stitch. Do this by drawing a loop through the nearest underarm stitch and passing this loop over the final sleeve stitch. Do it at the end of every sleeve row until all the underarm stitches are used up, at which point the sleeve automatically comes together in the center of the underarm and may be continued in rounds or rows, whichever you prefer. The bottom of the sleeve is thus knitted into the cast-on edge without any sewing. Of course, if you prefer to sew the sleeve to the body at the underarm, just work the sleeve in rows until it is more than long enough to reach across the underarm opening, then sew it in place.

This design is as easy to wear as it is to make. The shoulder is roomy, and the sleeve fits with remarkable grace, considering that its cap was never shaped at all. The secret of this comfortable fit is the splayed underarm, which draws the upper part of the sleeve gently downward to a good sleeve's correct angle. Pattern and color decorations of all kinds can be added to call attention to the unusual shoulder lines, so this very simple style can create some of the most exciting knitwear. Try a square-set sleeve today!

✳ *VARIATION*

SHAPED SQUARE-SET SLEEVE. If you should want to add a little extra roundness to the cap of the square-set sleeve, combine its principles of design with those of the seamless set-in sleeve. These principles can be applied in varying degrees. For a lightly rounded shoulder, work a few short rows in the sleeve after picking up the sleeve stitches. Make the first turns on each side of the center third of the stitches, and subsequent turns at intervals of about $\frac{1}{2}''$ until all the sleeve stitches have been worked. For a rounder shoulder, turn at intervals of $\frac{1}{4}''$. Or, you can make a regular set-in sleeve cap by turning in the usual way, one stitch at a time all the way down to underarm level, still keeping the square-set underarm instead of the usual curve.

Figure 78.
Dropped-Shoulder
Ski Sweater

BASIC DESIGN NO. 11

Dropped-Shoulder Ski Sweater

This is the simplest sweater shape ever invented. Its traditional from-the-bottom-up version was invented so long ago that its origin is lost in the mists of time. The body is a large unshaped tube; the sleeves are two smaller tubes attached to the upper corners of the large one. Since there is no shoulder shaping, the sleeve "caps" consist of those portions of the body that hang down over the shoulders. Consequently the join between body and sleeve is not on the shoulder, but somewhere between shoulder and elbow.

In its original form, the sweater was worked by knitting a seamless body-tube from lower edge to neck, and then slashing openings for the sleeves, which could be worked either from the top down or from the bottom up. Sleeves worked from the top down began with stitches picked up around the slashed armhole opening. Sleeves worked from the bottom up were knitted to the correct length, then sewn or woven or knitted into the armhole. The garment's extremely simple, boxlike lines lend themselves to lavish enrichment of the fabric with many colorful patterns.

The dropped shoulder is still popularly used for sportswear, and is usually worked in the traditional way, with armholes machine-stitched and slashed. Some knitters are nervous about this slashing operation, though, and tend to shy away from garments of this type because of it. Such knitters will be happy to know that this seamless from-the-top version involves no cutting. Beginners who have not yet gone very far with shaping will enjoy this design, because it really doesn't have to be shaped at all.

You will need a 29″ circular needle, a 16″ circular needle, and, if the sleeves are to be seamless, a set of sock needles. A 24″ needle or a pair of straight needles

101

will be handy, too, in case you want to start the sleeves before closing the body sections into a tube.

Begin by measuring the full circumference of the body, allowing for ease. Divide this measurement by 2 and multiply by your stitch gauge. This is the number of stitches to be cast on for the back. With a long piece of string and the 29" needle, invisibly cast on this number of stitches and start knitting a perfectly straight piece, long enough to reach from the top of the shoulder to about 2" below the underarm. Or, to put this instruction in a different way, simply knit the back as long as half a sleeve width. Leave the back stitches on a string.

If you want to, you can put a couple of short rows across the shoulders, but the shoulders of this garment should not be given more than a very slight slope. It is natural for the "sleeve-cap" portions of the body to flare out over the arm before the sleeves are added; therefore a perfectly straight shoulder will fit as well as any.

For the front, take the stitches of the left shoulder from their cast-on string onto the needle, skip the neck opening, and take the stitches of the right shoulder onto the same needle; work the shoulder fronts with two balls of yarn, just like a sleeveless sweater. To determine how many stitches should be omitted in the center for the neck opening, multiply the desired breadth of the neck opening by your stitch gauge, subtract this from the total number of stitches on the back section, and divide by 2. This tells you how many stitches should be worked on each shoulder front.

Make the front neck shaping just like that of a sleeveless sweater, rounding the corners at the neck edges with increases if you wish. In some of its more traditional versions, this sweater is not rounded at the front of the neckline, but worked with a high square neck, which appears rounded after a round neckband is added to it. To work it in this way, do not use any increases. Knit the neck edges straight down until they have come to the level of the throat, then cast on all the neck stitches straight across and join the left and right sections together.

Continue to work the front for as many rows as the back, without any shaping. This makes a wide rectangle with a neck-hole in the middle—and a neckband too if you have finished it. From here you can proceed in one of two ways. You can start the sleeves now, and work on them for a while before putting the front and back sections of the body together. Do this simply by picking up the desired number of sleeve stitches along the side edge of the rectangle, and start working a sleeve—in rows, on straight needles, or in rounds, on a 16" needle, whichever you prefer. Or, you can ignore the sleeves for the moment and continue working the body as a seamless tube. Do this by putting the back and front sections on the 29" needle and proceeding in rounds.

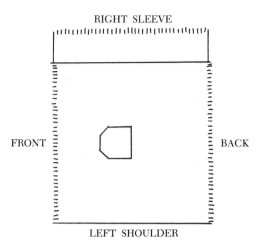

Figure 79. Top view of dropped-shoulder yoke, beginning right sleeve before joining body sections together

In the latter case, you have some scope for further width adjustments. If you think the body could use a little more width, cast on a few extra stitches at each underarm while working the first round. If you think the body could use a little less width, don't cast on any underarm stitches, but work a few decreases under each arm during the first few rounds. The traditional shape is perfectly straight, with stitches neither added nor subtracted. The lower part of the body can be tapered later, if you wish.

To add a sleeve, use the 16″ needle to pick up the desired number of sleeve stitches around the armhole, and start downward, working in rounds or rows. If the armhole has already been closed at the underarm, you will have to begin with a 16″ needle even if you are planning to work the sleeves in rows. Go back and forth around the armhole on the 16″ needle until the sleeve has grown enough to be placed on a longer circular needle or on a straight needle.

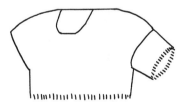

Figure 80. Dropped-shoulder yoke, beginning seamless sleeve after body sections have been joined together

To find out how many sleeve stitches should be picked up, measure loosely around the upper arm at the point where the dropped shoulder falls, and multiply by your stitch gauge. Taper the sleeve in the usual way with decreases between this point and the wrist. When you can see by trying on the garment that the sleeve is long enough, finish it off with a ribbed cuff, or a hem, or a patterned border, or whatever you like.

That's all. Isn't that an easy sweater design? Don't you think it odd that people should require knit-by-numbers directions to make such a sweater? Of course, the best part of a dropped-shoulder garment is the pattern work. The rich fabric interest typical of the traditional ski sweater is created by the interplay of patterns and colors, which embellish all those plain surfaces. Fair Isle knitting is the usual technique, but you don't have to stick to that. Slip-stitch color patterns and mosaic patterns can ornament your sweater just as well, and add texture excitement too, while giving you the ease of handling only one strand of yarn at a time. The same sweater shape can be made with cables and other textured patterns—even lace. Give your imagination free rein when working this simple design, and your sweater will be fun to knit and fun to wear.

✽ VARIATION

DROPPED SADDLE SHOULDER. Like any design that starts from a single cast-on row at the shoulder, and works in two directions, the dropped-shoulder

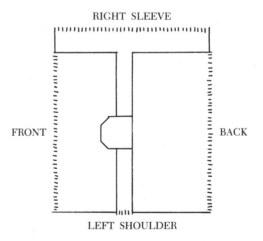

Figure 81. Top view of dropped saddle shoulder yoke,
beginning right sleeve on stitches picked up from side edge and saddle

garment can start with equal ease from the side edges of a saddle strip. Begin by measuring the desired body width from underarm to underarm; subtract the desired breadth of the neck opening, and divide by 2. Work each saddle strip until it is that many inches long, leaving the stitches on strings. Proceed as for a saddle-shoulder sweater, picking up the stitches of the back from the two saddles and casting on the neck stitches between them. After the front and back sections are joined together, start the sleeve by picking up the stitches from the saddle string, then picking up the rest of the sleeve stitches around the armhole. Thus the saddles will continue smoothly down into the sleeves without a break, so that you can work a pattern panel along each saddle strip and all the way down to the wrist. You can also work the saddles and sleeves in a different color from the rest of the body, which gives a very striking effect to a dropped-shoulder design.

Figure 82. Classic Cap

BASIC DESIGN NO. 12

Classic Cap

A cosy knitted cap is a comfort that almost every man, woman, and child needs and appreciates in wintry weather. It keeps the ears warm, and plays its part in warding off the common cold, as well as frostbite and other unpleasantnesses. It is a little thing, easily knitted up in an hour or two, but its usefulness is incalculable.

There are many different styles for knitted caps and hats. But in essence a cap is nothing but a head-sized tube, closed at one end. The classic ribbed cap is usually made from the bottom up by working a ring of ribbing, then decreasing the top to a few stitches, which are drawn together by the final yarn-end. The doubtful moment comes in deciding where to begin the decreases. If they are begun too soon, the cap will be too short, and will need constant tugging to remind it to cover the ears. If they are begun too late, the cap will be too long, and will either envelop the face or bag out at the back of the head. All doubt is eliminated, however, by working the cap from the top down. Once the top is shaped, you can easily see just how much knitting should be added to make the cap the right length.

To make a seamless cap, you will need a set of sock needles and a 16″ circular needle. Begin by casting 8 stitches onto one of the double-pointed needles. Divide these 8 stitches on 3 needles and join them together, making sure that they are not twisted. Take the fourth double-pointed needle and knit the first round by increasing 1 stitch in each of the 8 stitches, making a total of 16. Work one round even. Then work a second increase round, as follows: *increase in the first stitch, k1; repeat from * around. Now there are 24 stitches. Work another round even,

106

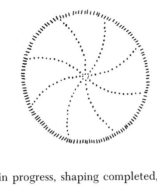

Figure 83. Top view of cap in progress, shaping completed, ready to work straight ribbing

then a third increase round: *increase in the first stitch, k2; repeat from *. This makes 32 stitches. Continue increasing 8 stitches every other round, having one more stitch between increases each time. Fourth increase round: *increase in the first stitch, k3; repeat from *. Fifth increase round: *increase in the first stitch, k4; repeat from *. And so on.

If you want to make the entire cap in a ribbed pattern, develop the ribbing between increases instead of knitting plain. As you proceed, you will see that the increases form 8 swirled lines on a disc of knitting. This disc is the top of the cap. When it is big enough to cover the crown of the head, like a beanie, stop increasing and work the cap as a straight tube in any ribbing pattern. Whenever there are enough stitches to go around the 16″ needle, you can change to this and lay the double-pointed needles aside. Any time you want to try on the cap, put some of the stitches on a string or on another circular needle of any length, returning them to the 16″ needle for working.

If you don't want a turned-up cuff, just work down to earlobe level and bind off. The classic ski cap, with a cuff, is ribbed for about 7″ past the end of the increases, or for a total length of about 10″ or 11″. To finish the top of the cap, draw the original 8 stitches tightly together with the yarn-end left over from casting on, and fasten off. Add a pompon, or a button, or a knitted flower, or any other decoration that you like. (What's the easiest way to make a knitted flower? Garter stitch petals—a small pompon center—sew them together!)

* VARIATIONS

SEAMED CAP. A cap with one seam can be worked in rows on straight needles— or, for easier in-progress fitting, on a 29″ circular needle. Start by casting on 8 stitches and increasing every right-side row, just as for the seamless cap. A long yarn-end left over from casting on may be used to sew the seam on the wrong side down to the turn of the cuff, and the yarn-end left over from binding off may be used to sew the seam inside the cuff, which is, of course, the reverse side of the fabric.

NARROW-CROWN CAP. When working the top of a cap in stockinette stitch instead of ribbing, it is customary (though not essential) to work 7 increases per increase round, instead of 8. This gives a more domelike shape to the top. Begin by casting on 7 stitches and immediately increasing to 14; thereafter, increase 7 stitches every other round in the usual way.

STOCKING CAP. A seamless stocking cap is worked like an endless sock, on double-pointed needles, with increase rounds spaced very far apart. This tube is pointed at the starting end, and gradually develops enough stitches to go around the head, finishing with ribbing. A seamed stocking cap is the same thing, worked as a slowly-widening strip instead of a tube.

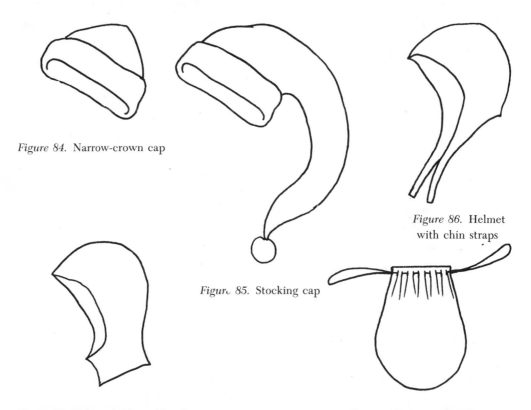

Figure 84. Narrow-crown cap

Figure 86. Helmet with chin straps

Figure 85. Stocking cap

Figure 87. Helmet with neckband

Figure 88. Drawstring bag

HELMET WITH CHIN STRAPS. Having worked the cap to hairline level, put the stitches on a piece of string and try it on. Place 4 markers of contrasting-colored yarn into the edge, about 1″ before and behind each ear. Return the stitches to the needle and bind off the back-neck section and the front section, but not the ear sections between the markers. Continue working each of these sections in rows, in a non-curling pattern stitch, decreasing 1 stitch each side every third or fourth row. When the strap has come down to a width of about 1″, work even until it is long enough to pass under the chin. Short straps can be secured under the chin with a button; longer straps can be tied. This is an excellent design for a baby cap. The first time you make it for a baby, though, do it while the baby is available for fitting. There isn't much space between a baby's ear and jaw, and you may find it necessary to decrease the straps over the ears quite rapidly.

HELMET WITH NECKBAND. To add a neckband to your helmet instead of straps, place the markers in front of the ears but none in back. Bind off the front of the cap, then work the entire back of the neck in rows with ribbing, decreasing at front edges and at the center back. When the front edges have come down below the jawline, cast on enough stitches to reach across the front of the neck, join all stitches together on the 16″ needle, and work in rounds until the neckband is the desired length.

DRAWSTRING BAG. Try a new experience in knitting, by working a cap in material other than yarn, and using it upside-down as a bag. String, straw, jute, twine, mason's line, fishline, heavy button-and-carpet thread, macramé cord, fancy Christmas-package cord, or any other type of cord can make a good bag. Strong braided-nylon fishline or nylon kite string will make an admirably weatherproof and durable clothespin bag, beach bag, fish net, fruit bag, or even a rock bag—for amateur geologists. Metallic cord will make a pretty little evening bag. If you're a string-saver, use some of your savings to knit little string bags for the children to carry their inevitable collections of small hard objects. For some reason, most small children love to keep their collections of small hard objects in drawstring bags.

Follow directions for the cap, using stockinette stitch or any other pattern stitch that you like. When the bag is long enough, thread the stitches with two drawstrings; or, work a final round of eyelet holes, bind off, and thread the drawstrings through the holes.

How to Match Patterns

Remarks under Basic Design #4, the seamless skirt (page 55), have already indicated several methods of matching stitch patterns across shaping lines. Pattern-matching is important, not only in skirts, but in all garments wherever it is possible. Just as mismatched stripes or plaids at the seams of a sewn garment jar the beholder with their crude, sloppy appearance, so mismatched knitting patterns detract from the perfection of a hand-knit. Time spent on planning the manipulation of pattern stitches, so that they develop evenly on adjacent garment sections, is perhaps the most vital time in any designing project.

Of course when you are knitting from the top, you should never have any difficulty in matching pattern *rows* on different sections of the garment. Back, front, and sleeve sections begin at the same place, so each of them can be started with the appropriate pattern row. Matching pattern *stitches* is a more exacting procedure, but easy enough to accomplish in most cases.

Side lines, raglan lines, under-sleeve lines, front edges of cardigans, crotch and leg seams of pants, all should have patterns accurately matched on each side so that the design is symmetrical. This is simple to manage on two adjacent sections that are worked alike, such as the back and front of a sweater, or the left and right sides of pants. To plan the patterning for pants, all you have to do is place the *center* of a pattern repeat at each side "seam." Then the patterns will automatically match across the crotch shaping, no matter how many stitches are added to each side by the double increases. Back and front sections of garments always should have centered patterns. Since each of these sections has the same number of stitches, they will be patterned alike, each side of the center, and will therefore match at the sides even where partial repeats are worked to maintain the correct width, or where the sides of the garment are tapered. Dart shaping will be patterned symmetrically, too, since each dart is worked the same number of stitches away from the center. An under-sleeve seam will automatically match if the pattern is centered on the sleeve section.

Since the front of a garment has no center until the neck shaping is finished, you have to arrange the pattern on its shoulder portions by copying from the back. If the front patterns match the back patterns at each side, then the front is bound to be correctly patterned when the front neck cast-on brings the stitches to the same total as the back. The left and right front sections of a cardigan are also copied from the back, so that the front edges will be patterned alike (in reverse) no matter what kind of sleeve shaping is used.

Seamless circular knitting possesses an inherent potential for beautiful pattern arrangement that no other method of garment construction can duplicate: it can repeat the same pattern continuously around the circumference of the garment without a break anywhere. This exquisite refinement is very simply achieved, just by making sure that the tube contains an exact multiple of the stitches required to form the pattern—no more and no less. When planning the body of a seamless garment, you have only to ask yourself, "How many pattern repeats will give me the width I want?" Then use that number of repeats to make continuous patterning that cannot help drawing attention to the garment's cleverly-designed seamlessness.

When casting on stitches at the underarm, to begin working down the lower body of your garment, try to cast on the right number of stitches to fill out one or two more exact pattern multiples, so the pattern will come out even all the way around. This may not be possible in a case where one pattern repeat has a large number of stitches. One more full pattern repeat on each side may make the garment too wide; one less may make it too narrow. But *think* about it, every time, and do it if you can. The craftsmanlike beauty of a seamless garment with continuous patterning is worth striving for, even if you have to settle for an inch more or an inch less than the width that you had in mind.

Very often you can cast on more than an exact multiple of stitches at the underarms, to allow for the extra ease that is required there, and taper the sides of the garment down to exact multiples later. The gusset under a kimono sleeve can be managed in this way; so can raglans and sleeveless-sweater shapes with all their sleeve variations. When the extra stitches have been decreased away, stop decreasing and let the pattern run unbroken around each side of the garment.

When planning lower borders and seamless sleeve cuffs for pattern stitches different from those in the body, be sure to decrease enough stitches, before starting the border, so that the border pattern will have its own exact multiple. Seamless waistbands and neckbands should show continuous patterning, too. Collars, like the front edges of a cardigan, should match on each side. This is easily done by centering the collar pattern at the back of the neck.

To match patterns across raglan seams, it is necessary not only to center the pattern on each front, back, and sleeve section, but also to make sure that there are equal numbers of stitches in the partial repeats on each side of each seam stitch. This planning is done at the start. Once you get the patterns matched across the raglans on the first row, they will automatically increase evenly when each subsequent increase is a double one. The initial matching may necessitate a half-inch less on back and front sections or a half-inch more on sleeve sections, or vice versa. But raglan yoke sizes are surprisingly adaptable, and further width adjustments can always be made at the underarms. Even if you have to start with a neck-back $6\frac{1}{2}''$ wide instead of the $6''$ that you wanted, it's worth it to achieve pattern matching over the raglans. In such a case, you can always narrow the neck later by picking up fewer stitches for the back of the neckband. Knitting is so flexible a medium that you can move stitches around, and add or subtract some here and there, with much greater impunity than most novice knitters realize.

Pattern charting on graph paper is the handiest way I know to pre-plan garments with accurately matched patterns. Methods of charting have been exhaustively described in a previous book, *Charted Knitting Designs*, so I won't attempt to go into the subject again, here. However, charting should be mentioned in this context. The shape of any garment section can be drawn on graph paper with every stitch and pattern operation in its proper place, which helps the knitter to visualize the arrangement of the pattern on every row, along with any kind of shaping, increase or decrease. For instance, the upper parts of a raglan yoke can be drawn by sections, each section increasing in width by one square every time a new stitch is added, with the pattern centered on the right number of squares. The widening sides of each section chart show how the pattern should be planned to match the similarly widening sides of adjacent sections.

There is one more refinement essential to the beautiful appearance of a well-designed hand-knit, and that is the blending of garment patterns with border patterns whenever possible. A sweater containing cables and bordered with ribbing, for instance, should always continue the cable ribs smoothly into the border, without allowing the purl stitches of the ribbing to break into the knit stitches of the cables and chop them short. This is more easily accomplished in knitting from the top than in knitting from the bottom, since the final border can be planned to suit patterns that are already established. An increase-and-decrease round, inserted between body patterns and border, is what bridges the stitch-count gap between the two.

For example, a certain section of the garment might have two cable ribs of three stitches each, with four purl stitches between them. To blend this into a border of k2, p2 ribbing, you might k2 tog and k1 in each of the cables, and p2 tog twice between, which smoothly decreases 10 garment stitches into 6 ribbing stitches. In another section, there might be a single knit stitch with two purl stitches on either side of it; you could increase 1 stitch in the knit stitch, thus converting 5 garment stitches into 6 ribbing stitches. The increase-and-decrease round is very flexible, and does *not* have to result in the same number of border stitches as there were garment stitches. Ribbings, especially in cable sweaters, are worked on about 10% fewer stitches than the body, more or less. There isn't any hard-and-fast formula for blending patterns into borders, because the proportions are different for every garment and every pattern combination. But it isn't difficult to work out; so *don't* be satisfied just to work down to a multiple of 4 stitches and then begin working k2, p2 ribbing without any regard to the placement of the patterns above. Proper blending makes a world of difference in the finished appearance of your garment.

Seamless garments worked from the top are knitted partly in rows and partly in rounds. Any pattern stitch can be worked in both straight and circular knitting, and most patterns are very easily converted from one to the other, so you should not have any difficulty in passing from the "row" portions to the "round" portions. To change rows into rounds, simply work the wrong-side rows inside-out and backward. That is, read all knit stitches as purl stitches and vice versa; read all "slip one with yarn in back" stitches as "slip one with yarn in front" stitches and vice versa. Reverse the order of knitting operations so that the "wrong-side" round begins at the *end* of the row—which is, of course, the right-hand side of a flat piece. Since circular knitting always works from right to left, *all* pattern rows must progress from right to left, never returning from left to right as a wrong-side row does.

Most wrong-side rows are comparatively simple, because most pattern operations take place on right-side rows. You can re-write your pattern stitch for circular knitting, if this will help make it clearer, turning the wrong-side rows around as you write; or, you can chart the pattern as it appears from the right side of the fabric, and work in rounds according to the chart. You won't know how easy it is to convert any given pattern from rows to rounds until you've tried it, so try it by all means. (See also "Adapting Patterns for Circular Knitting," *A Second Treasury of Knitting Patterns*, p. xxix.) Like most of the principles in knitting, that of straight-to-circular conversion is readily grasped through the exercise of ordinary common sense. It doesn't require any mysterious inspiration from outer space, or any great gifts of intellect not vouchsafed to plain folks. All you have to do is reason your way through calmly to the right answer, just like adding up a column of grocery prices.

Correct shaping is an essential part of any garment, of course. But correct patterning is the master-touch that makes all the difference between a clumsy, amateurish garment and a superbly crafted one. When shape and pattern are happily wedded, each enhancing the other, the result is knitting at its best, more interesting in both concept and execution than any other kind of garment construction. It's a matter of give and take: you can adjust the shape to the pattern, or adjust the pattern to the shape, or a little of both. In the end, they should look made for each other—and you will be the one who made them that way.

Assorted Helpful Hints
and Other Miscellany

To prevent looseness of stitches between the needles when working a tube on double-pointed sock needles, simply knit 3 or 4 stitches into the next needle before starting to use the free needle. This changes the positions of the openings between needles to different locations in the tube, on every round. Any stitches that were stretched or loosened on one round will smooth up nicely on the next.

To bind off the last stitch of a seamless, circular-knit tube so that no jog or join is visible, do it like this. Draw the yarn-end *upward* through the last bound-off loop. With a yarn needle, pass the yarn-end *around* the two strands of the first bound-off loop (which lies over the second stitch of the final round). Then pass the yarn-end *downward* into the same bound-off loop from which it emerged. Fasten off on the wrong side. This makes the yarn-end form a horizontal loop just like all the others, uniting the bound-off edge smoothly and continuously so that no one can tell where the bind-off began or ended.

In the same fashion, you can join the side edges of a piece worked in rows, such as a sleeve. Leave a long yarn-end with which to sew the seam. Unite the last bound-off loop with the first, as above, thus drawing the edges together. Then continue to sew the seam with the same strand. (See information on sewing seams, Basic Design #1, page 27.)

To bind off an edge tightly, don't work the stitches while binding off. Leave the yarn hanging, and bind off by *slipping* all the stitches, one at a time. Slip 2 stitches to the right-hand needle point, then * pass the first stitch over the second. 115

Slip another stitch to the right-hand needle point, and repeat from * until all stitches are bound off.

To bind off an edge loosely, work the stitches with a large-sized needle, or make a yarn-over every three or four stitches and immediately bind off the yarn-over as if it were an extra stitch.

To bind off the last corner stitch on a border or neckband in such a way that the corner does not stick out, bind off all but the last stitch, so that you still have one (bound-off) stitch on the right needle point, and one (not bound-off) stitch on the left needle point. Slip the stitch from the right needle to the left needle. Now there are two on the left needle; pass the second (i.e., the last) stitch over the first. With a yarn needle, draw the yarn through the remaining stitch, which is the next-to-last one.

To join cast-on stitches firmly into a ring, or to join newly cast-on stitches to existing ones as at a pullover neck front or underarm, try clustering the two end stitches together. With yarn in front, slip one stitch from the left needle point to the right needle point. Pass yarn to back. Slip *two* stitches from the right needle point to the left needle point. Pass yarn to front. Slip *one* stitch to the right needle point again, which is where this stitch began in the first place. Insert the round marker if you are working a tube, and proceed with the round.

To join new skeins of yarn into the knitting, you can go to great lengths to avoid tying knots, as many knitters do in their anxiety to obey the unwritten law that says No Knots! Or, you can take the law into your own hands and tie knots anyway, provided you do it correctly. Terrible as this confession may seem, I'm of the Knot persuasion. I've tried splicing, both with and without thinning away some of the plies; I've tried knitting a stitch or stitches with both strands together; I've tried running one strand through the other. I still prefer knots.

This is my method: knit to the last 3″ of the old strand, drop it on the wrong side, take up the new strand and continue knitting, leaving another 3″ tail also on the wrong side. After working several inches more along the row, tie the two tails together in a firm square knot, drawing the knot up carefully so that it is exactly centered on the running-thread between the two stitches. A knot placed like this will never show on the right side. Run the two tails through the wrong side of the knitting in opposite directions, which secures the knot forever.

Beginners are often told to join new strands with knots at the side edges of the knitting. I *never* do this. It makes an ugly lump at the side edge and prevents easy, smooth sewing of the seam. It also wastes yarn. I always place a knot in the middle of a row, between two right-side knit stitches (or wrong-side purl stitches), keeping it well away from yarn-over holes or other special pattern operations. I run the two tails upward and downward from the knot, keeping them behind purl stitches on the wrong side and passing them under every *other* purl bump. This makes a secure and invisible finish that doesn't split any of the yarn and is easily unraveled if necessary.

To re-use wool, unravel the knitting by winding the yarn around a broad object, such as an ironing board or a chair back, until the hank is about an inch thick. Tie the hank loosely in four or five places with short lengths of string, and wash it. All the kinks will disappear as if by magic. Let the hanks drip-dry for several days, until the last trace of dampness is gone. You can re-wind each hank into a ball for knitting, or knit right from the hank itself, by laying it out carefully in a circle and removing the strings. There it must stay undisturbed until it is all used, so don't try this in a household containing kittens, puppies, small children, or guests who are likely to be careless about where they sit.

My method of washing wool hanks is unorthodox enough to give some people the horrors, but I'll describe it anyway. I fill a basin or pail with water that is not warm, but steaming hot. I fling the hanks in, and let them stay there for ten minutes, stirring occasionally. Then I hang them on a clothesline (out of the sun) by their strings, and let them drip. I do this awful thing because I have discovered that hot water shrinks the wool just enough to make it firmer and stronger than new. Naturally I would not wash a *garment* in hot water, and neither would you. Loose wool, however, always seems to come out considerably improved by the hot-water ordeal. But don't try it on synthetics. It won't help them a bit.

To prevent white or pale-colored yarns from becoming grubby during the knitting, because of contact with hands, furniture, and clothing, keep your knitting in a clean pillowcase. Spread the pillowcase over your lap, inside-out, while working. Wash your hands before knitting, and also during the work if the weather is warm and the hands, consequently, become sticky.

To keep the right side of a piece of circular knitting clean, work it inside-out. That is, have the loop of the circular needle toward you instead of away from you. You work on the right side of the fabric, as usual, but only the wrong side is exposed to your lap. In knitting from the top, finished sleeves can be tucked into the upper portion of the garment while you are working on the lower portion. This makes a nice compact package of the work, and keeps the sleeves clean.

Always keep a nail file and manicure scissors or nail clippers in your knitting bag. The tiniest nick on the edge of a fingernail, or a roughness of skin on the finger, or an almost imperceptible hangnail can snag your yarn. If the tools are handy to repair any "catch" on your hand, you won't be tempted to just sit there and live with it, rather than getting up to fetch your manicure implements.

Never hang a hand-knitted garment on a clothes hanger, unless you want it to lengthen. When you put it away, fold it and lay it flat. If you want to be really fussy, you can bolster the folds with crushed tissue paper, but this isn't necessary if you fold with care.

To take the curls out of a new nylon circular needle, or an old one that has been stored away coiled up, hold it stretched and pass it back and forth under hot running water a few times.

To pick apart a hard knot with ease, use the point of a yarn needle as a fid. What is a fid? It's a pointed tool used by sailors to pick apart hard knots in rope, or to open the strands for splicing. It's surprising how quickly a knot will collapse, once you get a smooth pointed instrument under one of the strands.

To wind yarn into a ball that pulls from the middle, just hold the end of the yarn on your palm, exposed, while you wind the ball over your fingers. Wind the yarn loosely, and don't lose that yarn-end. It will pull out of the ball quite pleasantly, giving you a ball that is stable and won't bob around, as it does when the yarn is pulled from the outside of it. In a situation where you haven't much yarn left and want to divide it evenly between two scarf-ends or sleeve-cuffs or pant-legs that are being worked at the same time, row for row, you can knit both ends of the yarn at once by pulling from the middle *and* the outside of the ball. The two strands will tend to become twisted from time to time, but you won't mind this if you're really desperate to use every inch of it in matching halves.

To wind a hank into a ball, you don't really need an assistant holding up a pair of tired arms, and grumbling. Just drop the hank over something vertical and without projections, such as a small upside-down stool, the back of a straight chair, the cat's scratching-post, or a cardboard coat-box held upright between your feet. Stand up above this object and draw the yarn straight up to the ball.

To separate the plies of a strand of yarn, in order to get thinner yarn of the same color and dye lot, pull out a five-foot length of yarn from the ball and then put a rubber band around the ball. Open the plies and hold them apart above your head, one section in each hand, so that the ball hangs clear of the floor. Let the yarn untwist down to the ball, then repeat the process with another five-foot length. You can untwist longer lengths, each time, by standing up on a chair or a ladder—or you can untwist very long lengths by dropping the ball out of a second-story window or down a stair-well.

Did you ever try making a felted coat or jacket, for really efficient cold-weather insulation? It's not so hard to do. Make a test swatch of wool, wash it in very hot water and tumble-dry, so that it shrinks as far as it can. Take your stitch and row gauge from this shrunken swatch rather than from the actual knitting. The garment will seem big enough to fit King Kong, until you subject it to the same shrinking treatment and bring it down to size. After shrinking, the fibers will be matted together, making a warm, durable, windproof garment.

Well-felted knitting can be cut and sewn like a woven fabric, because the matted fibers will not allow it to unravel. It makes sturdy blankets, slippers, and handbags. Felting is also a good last-resort solution to the problem of an adult-size sweater that the adult wearer doesn't wear or doesn't like. Shrink it, and then try it on one of the children. It's bound to fit *some*body. And, being felted, it will keep the one it fits very warm indeed.

To knit easily with any material that comes on a spool, such as ribbon, string, thread, or cord, put the spool in a cardboard box of appropriate size and skewer it on a double-pointed needle thrust through the sides of the box. Use a needle small enough in diameter so the spool will turn freely on it. Secure the points of the needle by wrapping and re-wrapping them with rubber bands just outside the box. With this arrangement, you can pull the strand off the spool smoothly, without any turns, twists, or kinks.

To line or not to line? Some people do, and some don't. I don't, as a general rule. As a devotee of seamless knitting and a seeker of the ultimate in flexibility, I feel that linings detract from the natural suppleness of knitted garments. To affix knitting to pieces of yard goods is to treat the knitting as if it *were* yard goods, and to ignore its special, unique characteristics. A properly constructed lining does help the garment to retain its shape—that is, to retain the shape of the lining. But if the right shape is knitted into the garment in the first place, the innate springiness of the knitting will retain it.

Sometimes, though, you may want to make partial linings. If your skin is irritated by wool, you can still wear woollen coats and jackets by adding strips of lining inside neckbands and cuffs, where the garment touches the skin. Lining strips can be used to correct droopy front bands, too-long shoulder seams, or over-large neckbands: cut the strip to the right length and tack the knitting to it, drawing stitches or rows in to fit. Interfacing fabric, netting, stretch seam binding, or ordinary gauze bandage can be used for this purpose. Pockets may be lined to take the strain off the knitting when the pocket carries something. Zipper plackets may be lined to keep the edges firm. However, I don't use linings or interfacings just to give body to collars, cuffs, lapels, pocket flaps, and other ornamental touches. I prefer to knit these touches in some firm, flat, dense pattern stitch that has its own built-in body, without non-knitted additions.

Lace garments are often lined, but I like to leave them unlined and wear them over matching or contrasting-colored undergarments. A full lining, when constructed with true attention to detail, should be carefully tacked to the knitted garment all over, by hand. This rather tedious process can do odd things to knitted lace, so that it looks less attractive than it would look if left alone.

Lining enthusiasts must forgive me if my remarks on lining seem to be mostly advice on how to avoid lining. But for those who think knitting is more fun than sewing, and who therefore look upon lining as useless drudgery, these remarks may provide some assurance that they are not alone.

INDEX